ORANGERIES

Acknowledgements
The authors thank Hervé Burdet, Laurent de Froberville, Bertrand Guillou, Jannick Guillou, Catherine Jumel, Jean-Paul Médard, Michel de Pontville, Edmond de Rothschild, Guy de Vendeuvre, Marie-José Villadier, Francis Villadier, Giovanni Giordano, Michele Longo, Valentino Longo, Katharina Bott, Beat Preschel, Karl von Schönborn, Heide Vogt, Sarah Bullen, Ian Cadogan, Patsy Cullen, Peter Day, Lord Faringdon, Kate Fielden, Elisabeth Greenwood, Myles Thoroton Hildyard, Peter Robinson, Lord Somerleyton, Lord Shelburne, Carol Smith, Dominick Spencer, Michael Szell, Henry R. Tempest and Jean Bianca Wyat for their hospitality, their kindness and their help, and Lionel Saudan and Christophe Saudan for their participation.

Pages 4–5:
Park of Sans-Souci
Potsdam, Brandenburg
Orangery Palace
© Monheim/von Götz, ARCHITEKTON

EVERGREEN is an imprint of Benedikt Taschen Verlag GmbH

© for this edition: 1998 Benedikt Taschen Verlag GmbH
Hohenzollernring 53, D–50672 Köln
© 1994 ATELIER D'ÉDITION «LE SEPTIÈME FOU», Geneva
Text, illustrations, layout and conception: Michel Saudan and Sylvia Saudan-Skira, Geneva
Translation: Alayne Pullen in association with First Edition Translations Ltd., Cambridge, UK
Cover: Angelika Taschen, Cologne

Printed in Spain
ISBN 3-8228-7765-4
GB

SYLVIA SAUDAN-SKIRA
MICHEL SAUDAN

ORANGERIES

PALACES OF GLASS – THEIR HISTORY AND DEVELOPMENT

EVERGREEN

Contents

I

THE PURSUIT OF PLEASURE

Creating new environments to delight the senses

When the young Florentine Giovanni Boccaccio returned from the king-dom of Naples in 1340, he brought with him dazzling memories of gardens heavy with the perfumes of the Orient and of palaces where the court of Robert of Anjou still perpetuated the refinement and sensual delight of the last Aghlabite caliphs.

At the Villa Palmieri, among the hills of Fiesole, the poet regaled his friends, who already yearned for a new golden age, with descriptions of land-scapes where "a meadow of smooth grass, so dark as to appear black, stretched forth, scattered with a profusion of many-coloured flowers. Orange and citron trees surrounded it with their deep, bright green. Still in blossom, though hanging with fruit both old and new, they delighted the eyes with their shade and their sweet fragrance."[1]

It was in fact from the Orient – in the wake of the Arab conquest of Spain and then of Sicily during the eighth and ninth centuries – that two new, sweetly scented fruit trees were introduced into Andalusia and south-ern Italy – the lemon tree (*Citrus limonum*) and the sour or Seville orange (*Citrus aurantium bigaradia*). Although these trees, like the bay and the pomegranate, had graced the gardens of Baghdad and Damascus they had remained unknown in the countries of the Mediterranean, as had the differ-ent cultivated species of the *Citrus*, except the citron (*Citrus medica*).[2]

These two fruit trees, native to Burma and the plains of Hindustan, had been introduced into Mesopotamia centuries earlier. In the fifth century BC they were given names by the Persians from which many of the names they would later receive derive: *laymn* in Persian became *limone* in Italian, *lemon* in Spanish and *limon* in French. The latter was gradually replaced by the word *citron* which until then had referred only to the citron itself. In the same way the Persian word *nāran* gave rise, via Arabic, to *melarancio* and later *arancio* in Italy, *naranja* in Spain, and *orenge* in fifteenth-century France.[3]

Although, following the conquests of Alexander the Great, peach trees from Persia, apricot trees from Armenia and plum trees from Anatolia bloomed on the Peloponnese, the Greeks, and later the Romans, showed little interest in the lemon or the sour orange. Only the citron was brought back from Media by the Macedonian troops, and this mainly for its medi-cinal properties. The peel of the "apple of Media" or "Persian apple", as Theophrastus called it, was used to flavour wines recommended for arthritis. It was also prescribed as a digestive in the form of an infusion and, chewed, it had a reputation as a tonic.[4]

It seems likely that the bitter taste of the sour orange and the acidity of the lemon were the reasons for the lack of interest shown by the Greeks and Romans. In his treatise *Historia Naturalis*, Pliny describes the fruit as "despised by some due to their odour and bitterness". He also adds a warning concerning the difficulty of cultivating these fruits: "Some nations have attempted to cultivate the apple of Media in their own lands for its medicinal properties; it was transported in clay pots to allow aeration of the roots – a method worthy of note... However, the tree refused to grow outside Media and Persia."[5]

It was not until the first sweet-fruiting orange, *Citrus aurantium sinensis,* was brought back from the Far East by Portuguese navigators that those interested in rare fruit were ready to give full acceptance to the "orange apple", as it was then known. From the middle of the sixteenth century the art of "managing the citron, the lemon, and the orange"[6] was gradually accorded a more prominent position in agricultural treatises of the period.

These fruits were now divided into two distinct genera. On the one hand there was the *Citrus*, which at the time included the citron and the lemon, soon joined by, among others, the bergamot orange, a variety cultivated for its aromatic properties. On the other was the genus *Aurantium*, which at the time consisted only of the sweet orange and the sour orange. In Holland in 1665 the *pompelmoes* was added; this was discovered some ten years later by the French and named *pampelmous.* The varieties developed rapidly along with citrus cultivation as a whole and were given such evocative names as the "apple of Adam", the "horned orange", and even the "hermaphrodite orange". However, it was not until Carl von Linné that some order was brought to their classification and the various, and by now celebrated species were grouped together under one genus: the *Citrus.*[7]

Oranges and lemons now appeared on the tables of the rich. "The flowers of the lemon are eaten in salads, preserved in vinegar or with honey and sugar. Orange blossom is used to produce rare and precious scented waters. And we know how highly prized are fine, ripe oranges both on the banquet table and in preserves. Besides which the peel of the orange is used to flavour mustard, spice bread, and other delicacies..."[8]

Citrus trees were lovingly tended and, though valued for both their fruit and blossom,[9] it was their evergreen foliage that made them an indispensable ornament in the garden. They were grown in terracotta containers or in tubs rather than in the open ground as this was better suited to the composition of formal beds. As Agostino Gallo explains in *Le Venti giornate dell'agricoltura e dei piaceri della villa*, this enabled "the plants in their terracotta pots and containers to be maintained with such skill that not a single branch protruded beyond another and all who viewed them wondered at this display of power by Nature and Art working in harmony".

The balance and perfect harmony between Nature and Art, so sought after by the humanists, began, effectively, to force Nature to yield to the rules of Art. Soon, with a skilful sense of the dramatic, designers began to create gardens in a theatrical style with the different features of the decor, such as the steps, terraces, and fountains, highlighted by a variety of shadow. This ranged from the gentle shade cast by hedges of box and rosemary to the deeper shadow of avenues of cypress and the intermittent shade of rows of orange and lemon trees planted in containers.

With the adoption of these new designs a quick solution had to be found to the problem of where such tender plants, now an essential element of every garden, could be housed during the winter months. However, up to the eighteenth century in villas in Tuscany and the outskirts of Rome the trees in their containers were simply moved into converted storerooms next to the outbuildings or under the terraces for the cold season. They were also placed in open galleries or arbours enclosed with heavy wooden panels. Italy was in fact late in recognizing the need to provide a building specifically for the storage of tender fruit trees. Such buildings became known as *limonaia* since lemon trees were more commonly used than orange trees in the composition of formal beds. In fact it was not until 1785 that a man from the north, the Grand Duke Leopold I of Lorraine, son of the Empress Maria Theresa, introduced the *limonaia* to Tuscany, building an impressive example in the Boboli gardens.[10]

On the other side of the Alps the harsher climate compelled garden enthusiasts to find appropriate ways of protecting their delicate fruit trees. From the mid-sixteenth century noblemen, merchants, and medical botanists, in Germany, Flanders, and England in particular, arranged for the precious seeds of the orange to be brought from Genoa and Valencia.

Jan Commelin
Nederlantze Hesperides, 1676
Lemon blossom

Under northern skies the orange did not react well to frequent changes of position and in order to give the young trees the best chance of survival they were grown in the open ground rather than in pots and planted in two or three rows along a high, south-facing wall. However, this did not provide an adequate screen from the cold winds and frost of winter and a removable structure was designed to protect them from October to April. This, though costly and inconvenient,[11] was nevertheless the first form of shelter designed specifically for orange trees, and as such was the first step in the development of the orangery. It was a simple structure consisting of brick pillars or wooden posts supporting a frame covered by planks of oak and enclosed by panels of a similar nature. Any gaps were then "closed up and sealed with hay or tow". When the frosts came, one or more charcoal braziers were lit to maintain a temperature between 5 and 6° C (40 and 45° F). At the end of the winter one or two panels could be removed each day so that "the sun could shine on the plants and drive away the bad air, also eliminating the harmful humidity caused by the shade".[12]

In 1570 Duke Christoph von Württemberg, adopting this method for the protection of his orange trees in Stuttgart, became the first to introduce it in Germany. At the same period, and using the same method on his estate at Beddington, Sir Francis Carew became the first to succeed in growing orange trees in England. During the conquest of the kingdom of Naples and the "Italian campaigns" the French kings had also been captivated by the "Hesperidean" fragrance that filled the gardens from Campagna to Tuscany. Charles VIII wrote to his brother, "You cannot imagine the beauty of the gardens in this place, for, by my faith, only Adam and Eve are absent from this earthly paradise, so fine are these gardens and so filled with all things good and singular..."[13] Among the "singular things" brought back from Italy by Charles VIII in 1495 were the fruit trees for the châteaux on the banks of the Loire "that (the king) was then having newly and sumptuously built".[14] As early as 1517 the Cardinal of Aragon, visiting Blois, remarked on the presence of "A great number of lemon trees and large orange trees planted in wooden tubs".[15] And when, in 1522, François I confiscated the property of Charles of Bourbon, he had the collection of sour oranges that the duke was growing at great expense on his land at Chantelle brought to the gardens at Fontainebleau.

The fascination with Italy was not limited to the introduction of unfamiliar scents and flavours. Garden designers, of whom the most sought after were Italian, moved beyond the specific features of the model introduced from Italy by Pacello towards a more global concept of garden planning. They highlighted the importance of the interplay between terrace and loggia, introducing into their proposals something of "the effect" of which they were so fond, though the French were fearful of possible excesses.

In 1547 Philibert de L'Orme, who had just returned from three years in Italy, was engaged by Henri II to build the Château d'Anet and designed the orange garden the king wanted for his mistress, Diane de Poitiers, in this style. The "orangerie", as he called it – although the term still referred only to the formal garden – was surrounded by high walls and retained the charm of the medieval secret garden. However, a terrace overhanging it on one side made it possible to create an elegant arcaded gallery in the space below. This must have been intended for the winter storage of tender plants and was the forerunner of the royal orangeries that followed. Whether it was actually constructed or merely an architect's vision we cannot be sure as the only evidence that remains are the drawings.[16]

Some years later, in 1552, the Cardinal of Lorraine, Charles de Guise, who had just acquired the Château de Meudon, also adopted the terrace style, but throughout his gardens. The model for this came directly from Italy. Through his sister-in-law, Anne d'Este, the wife of François de Guise, the cardinal, by 1550, was aware of the grandiose plans – executed nine years later – that the duchess's brother, Cardinal Hippolyte d'Este, had for the development of his estate in Tivoli.

Charles de Guise requested the Italian designers working on the gardens and the famous grotto, designed by Primaticcio, to install "a porched area where orange trees could be placed" below one of the terraces. However, this could still not be described as a genuine orangery. Yet during the following century, when the new owner of the Château de Meudon, Abel Servien, Louis XIII's Secretary of State for War, was carrying out major improvements to the property he felt compelled – no doubt by the design of the gardens and the Italianate atmosphere that still prevailed – to order a "grand Orangery" to be built, giving it its formal title. This was a grandiose and original undertaking, almost certainly entrusted to Louis Le Vau, who was responsible for the renovation of the château, which, as recent studies show, was executed around 1658.[17] The high façade, punctuated with rustic bossage, had round-headed windows and French doors with square panes of glass and decorative glazing bars. The use of glass was unusual and replaced the simple trelliswork panels covered with gummed paper or oilcloth that were normally used to enclose arcades where container-grown plants were placed for the winter. Abel Servien had such an orangery built, and we now find the orange tree taking centre stage on a sumptuously decorated set provided specifically for it.

Not only had a specific environment been invented, but by the second half of the century the term *orangerie* was at last used not simply for "the garden in which orange trees are placed" but also for "an enclosed area designed for the storage of container-grown orange trees, where they may be kept safe from frost".[18] Nevertheless, the development of the orangery was slow, although some country gentlemen did begin to show an interest in the new concept, largely as a result of their connections with the countries of northern Europe. Among those close to the royal court the orangery continued to be considered principally as a formal garden and is referred to and highly recommended in treatises on "the art of gardening", including those written by Boyceau de la Baraudière and Claude Mollet.[19] However, with a few exceptions, the construction of an orangery was still a rare occurrence on royal estates. When one was built it was often little more than a simple gallery or large loggia adorning an orange garden, as was the case with the orangery built at the Château de Rueil for Cardinal Richelieu.

However, once Louis XIV became interested in it as an architectural feature it was not long before the orangery was in great demand among his entourage. With the death of Mazarin and the end of his regency, the king could no longer resist these legendary golden fruit said to have grown in the garden of the Nymphs of the Hesperides. What better symbol could there be of his now complete authority? It was not long before he followed the example of his Secretary of State and future minister, the Marquis de Louvois, who owned the magnificent orangery at the Château de Meudon, acquired in 1659. No sooner had Le Nôtre been commissioned to design the gardens at Versailles than Le Vau was summoned to collaborate in the construction of a Royal Orangery to rival the one at Meudon.

The palace's orangery was originally arranged on terraces, betraying a strongly Italian influence and the reawakening of the most fecund of myths, but between 1684 and 1686 it underwent a masterly transformation at the hands of Jules Hardouin-Mansart, who had taken charge of the work at Versailles in 1678. The orange trees, along with the pomegranate, myrtle, and bay, now had a palace of their own, a building with its own distinct characteristics. The façade consisted of two ell wings, 365 m (over 1,200 ft) in length, with impressive Tuscan order columns marking the entrances; there were French windows with double glazing, and immense rooms with vaulted ceilings capable of maintaining a temperature so constant that they did not require heating.

The example of Versailles was soon taken up by the rest of the court. In 1682 at Chantilly and in 1684 at Sceaux, André Le Nôtre and Jules Hardouin-Mansart were commissioned to build magnificent orangeries that would consist of both the building itself and the vast adjoining area of formal beds in which the orange trees were displayed. By the end of the century the orangery had become a necessary feature included in all the architectural treatises of the period.

Although, during the century that followed, the orangery rarely received the same degree of attention that it did under Louis XIV, it continued to give pleasure, though often more for its contents than for the charm of its architecture. The *Dictionnaire universel d'histoire naturelle* makes no mention of the orangery as a building but does, however, describe the orange tree as "the ornament of our most beautiful gardens, being cultivated in containers and protected in glasshouses from the severe winter weather".[20] Antoine Joseph Dezallier d'Argenville remarks in his work *Voyage pittoresque des environs de Paris* – published in 1755 – on the existence of orangeries in almost all the châteaux he visited. However, he is in fact often referring to the formal beds, of which he acknowledges the importance, and rarely to the "orange tree house", which according to him is "incorrectly known as an *orangery*, because this name should only be used for the garden where the container-grown orange trees are placed during the summer".

This metonymical transgression, which sometimes leads to confusion, could explain the relative enthusiasm with which this architectural development was greeted in France compared with England and Germany.

On the one hand the term "orangery" was too closely connected with container-grown plants and oranges in particular. These were fragile trees, often difficult to keep alive and heavy to move. Often "their weight made it impossible to carry them on stretchers and low trolleys moved by means of levers had to be employed".[21] One can imagine that estate owners might well have felt discouraged. In addition their regimented appearance – pruned into spheres and grown in containers – was increasingly out of harmony with the freedom of the open beds and borders filled with a profusion of different flowers that garden designers were now recommending, Dezallier d'Argenville being the first, in 1709.[22]

On the other hand the functional nature of the orangery meant that it was frequently treated as a purely utilitarian building. As with other outbuildings, such as the indoor manège or servants' quarters, the orangery was often situated to one side of the forecourt, not far from the kitchen garden. And although it may have graced the side terrace of a country mansion it was never incorporated into the woodland setting, the outdoor chambers or the trellised bowers that were features of the new and freer style of garden design. However, the orangery and its adjoining orange garden, consisting of formal beds, often with ornamental ponds and pathways of fine sand, required much greater care and attention than other outbuildings.

Too demanding to be used simply for pleasure and too sophisticated to be purely utilitarian, the orangery fell gradually into disuse. The Prince de Ligne himself, who was famous for his gardens at Belœil, fiercely criticized the building and its accompanying garden: "Orangeries", he wrote in 1781, "will always be in the ridiculous position of functioning neither as winter nor summer gardens."[23]

Moreover, by the end of the century the interests of the aristocracy had transferred themselves from the cultivation of the *Citrus* to other matters. The new fashion for "Anglo-Chinese" line drawing was accompanied by a fascination with botany and many began to collect the most exotic plants. Precious new species and varieties such as the scented acacia, the balsam, the amaranth, and the wild nutmeg tree were arriving in increasing numbers from overseas and new homes would have to be found to shelter them if gardens were to be the "land of experience" that their owners desired.

The nobility had also now rejected the charms of the orangery in favour of the simpler and more varied pleasures provided by small buildings such as temples of love, concert rooms, and pagodas, built as features in the new grounds of stately homes.

Jan Commelin
Nederlantze Hesperides, 1676
Orange blossom

Ornaments and Inspiration

In the sixteenth century, lemon and orange trees, which had now become a standard ornamental feature in the gardens of Tuscany, were also used to create atmosphere.

A year after his election as Duke of Florence in 1537, Cosimo I appointed Il Tribolo to redesign the gardens at Castello, the villa where he had spent his childhood, and recommended that one terrace be kept exclusively for lemon trees. His intention was to re-create, purely for the delight of the senses, the *locus amoenus* of which Lorenzo de Medici had been so fond a century earlier and the lemon trees in their serried ranks would play their part. With their fragrant shade, and gleaming foliage, the lemon trees prepared the visitor for the enchantment of the Grotto.

A quite different role was reserved for the orange tree in the magnificent Boboli gardens. Shortly after the accession to the throne of Cosimo II in 1609, Alfonso and Giulio Parigi began to transform the gardens into a vast theatre for the numerous festivities held by the grand duke. In 1618 Alfonso Parigi designed the breathtaking *Isolotto* to complete the main axis – the *Viottolone* – of the new garden. Out of reach on the small island situated in the centre of a large oval pool the "golden fruits of knowledge" were now no more than refined accessories. The gardens had lost their ritual power and were simply an elegant set with the orange trees forming part of the decor. Their terracotta pots surround Giambologna's majestic Ocean fountain, creating a counterpoint to the lightly curved balustrade.

ABOVE:
Giovanni Battista Ferrari
Hesperides sive malorum ..., 1646
Nymphs offering the golden apples ...
after a drawing by Pietro da Cortona

LEFT:
Villa de Castello
Tuscany
Il Tribolo and Bernardo Buontalenti
Gardens, 1538–1592
lemon tree beds

FACING PAGE:
Johann Christoph Volkamer
Continuation der Nürnbergischen Hesperidum, 1714
Garden of the Marchioness Spolverini, Verona

Giardino del Sig.r Marchese Spolverini, in Verona.

Giovanni Battista Ferrari
Hesperides sive malorum..., 1646

LEFT:
apple of Adam
FACING PAGE BELOW:
double flower oranges

<small>ABOVE AND FACING PAGE BELOW:</small>
Pitti Palace, Boboli Gardens
Florence
Alfonso Parigi
Isolotto, 1618

The New Gardens of the Hesperides

Before architects could make the orangery a more widespread feature of their programmes the cultivation of the *Citrus* had to cease to be the exclusive domain of monarchs and aristocrats. Interest among gardening enthusiasts was encouraged by works devoted to the subject and in 1536 a treatise by Charles Estienne, *De re hortensi libellus*, opened the way for publications on the cultivation of flowers and fruit trees for usefulness and pleasure, rather than works on agriculture in general. Education in "the art of garden cultivation" – which in 1631 was given the name *horticultura* by the German professor of botany Peter Lauremberg – attached increasing importance to the pruning and grafting of trees, thus encouraging the development of citrus cultivation as a speciality.

Many works on the subject appeared between 1640 and the start of the eighteenth century, often given the title *Gardens of the Hesperides*. Of these Giovanni Battista Ferrari's work was one of the most enchanting and complete.

Ferrari was a Jesuit priest and a professor of Hebrew and Arabic living in Rome. He had a passionate interest in horticulture, and called upon talented artists such as Guido Reni and Pietro da Cortona to provide the illustrations to his work. He was also innovatory in demonstrating with great care the different methods for protecting the trees currently in use in the gardens of the great prelates of Rome. Pergolas, used to grow plants in the open ground, were covered in winter with removable panels; a similar form of protection was used on arbours where citrons were grown as espaliers and bergamot oranges trained across the vaulted roofs; "orange tree rooms" – simple galleries with meshwork over the windows – were used for young plants and storerooms set aside for the over-wintering of container-grown orange trees.

However, it was the Dutch who were the greatest horticultural specialists of this period. Their new and powerful maritime trading companies – the Dutch East India Company and, from 1621, the West India Company – brought back vast numbers of new species to Holland.

Giovanni Battista Ferrari
Hesperides sive malorum..., 1646
after drawings by Philippe Gagliard

Above:
pergola with espalier citrons
Right:
vaulted room for young orange trees
Facing page:
arbour with bergamot oranges

Jan Commelin, a doctor and professor of botany at the University of Amsterdam, specialized in the development of the most modern horticultural methods. In 1676 he illustrated how new varieties of fruit could be obtained through the use of cuttings and grafting techniques, fruits such as "the sour orange with or without variegated leaves" and "the sweet orange with 'puffy' leaves". He also studied how these trees could be protected and proposed that a permanent shelter, to which he gave the name "winter garden", should be provided, rather than a temporary solution.

The Dutch style of orangery was already in use in the homes of some keen English and, occasionally, French gardeners; these were country gentlemen whose interest in this new type of building had been aroused by their familiarity with other northern countries. Jacques Moisant de Brieux was one of these: a lawyer at the Normandy parliament, in 1652 he founded the Caen Academy and was a forerunner of the eighteenth-century French intellectual. He travelled widely and, as a protestant, in Amsterdam and London made valuable contacts among notable specialists in citrus cultivation. As a result Brieux became one of the first gentlemen in France to build an orangery. He had acquired the estate of La Luzerne in 1637 and built his charming orangery with its tall, square-paned windows and a cornice adorned with vases.

Johann Christoph Volkamer, a wealthy Nuremberg merchant and owner of the finest orange garden in Bavaria, became famous with the publication of *Nürnbergischen Hesperidum*, which appeared between 1708 and 1714. Volkamer then commissioned the city's finest engravers to produce a series of engravings that he published under the title of *Continuation der Nürnbergischen Hesperidum*. The illustrations of each fruit were accompanied by views of stately homes in Germany, Austria, and Italy, making his work a rare and priceless record of garden design at that period.

Jan Commelin
Nederlantze Hesperides, 1676
Winter garden at the Leyden Academy

ABOVE:
façade
FACING PAGE BELOW:
interior

Manoir de La Luzerne
Bernières-sur-Mer, Normandy
Orangery, c. 1660

RIGHT:
cornice ornament,
depicting garden implements
FACING PAGE BELOW:
south-west façade

Francis van Sterbeeck
Citricultura, 1682

<small>Above left:</small>
training shrub trees
<small>Above:</small>
bay tree from the American Indies
<small>Left:</small>
aromatic bay
<small>Facing page:</small>
repotting

The Gardens in the Italian Style and Royal Orangeries

The new "Hesperidean" garden Louis XIV commissioned Le Vau to create at Versailles, in imitation of Abel Servien's orangery at Meudon, indulged his customary delight, here as elsewhere, of offering all while giving nothing. When first completed in 1664 the classic layout of the superb orange garden designed by Le Nôtre could be admired by all from the balustrade of the "parterre du Midi" or flower terrace.

Twenty years later the Orangery at Versailles was rebuilt and extended, revealing the king's intentions even more clearly. The new architect, Hardouin-Mansart, provided access to the garden by building the two monumental staircases known as the "One Hundred Steps", but surrounded the garden with high railings. Enclosed in this impressive "seraglio", access to the orange trees depended entirely on the goodwill of the king. Louis XIV – who in fact wrote a guide to the gardens entitled *Manière de montrer les Jardins de Versailles* – would lead his courtiers across the orange garden, which stood empty in winter, to the Salon de l'Orangerie, where they would gaze in wonder at this palace of oranges.

The king owed this extraordinary display to Jean-Baptiste de La Quintinie, who had been responsible for the fruit and vegetable gardens on the king's estates since 1670. La Quintinie was appointed to Versailles in 1661 and between 1678 and 1683 worked with Hardouin-Mansart on the new royal kitchen garden; this gave him the opportunity to experiment with new methods of transplanting, managing, and pruning fruit trees. In winter the orangery, to which the container-grown plants from the various royal residences were brought, housed more than 3,000 trees including oranges, lemons, bays, pomegranates, and thorn apples. Among these was the "Grand Connétable" or "Great Constable", the last sour orange in the collection of Duke Charles de Bourbon (who bore the title Constable), which was confiscated by François I.

Jean-Baptiste de La Quintinie
Le Parfait jardinier..., 1695

Above:
Orangery at Versailles
Facing page:
Creation of the formal beds

Left:
Château de Versailles
Jules Hardouin-Mansart
Orangery, 1684–1686
decorative vase on the gateway

Château de Meudon
Ile-de-France
Attributed to Louis Le Vau
Orangery, c. 1657–1658

Above:
general view
Facing page:
interior

Right:
L'Architecte, 1907
Restoration of the Château de Meudon in 1710

Château de Versailles
Jules Hardouin-Mansart
Orangery, 1684–1686

Above:
interior
Left:
side wing
Facing page:
rotunda room

Château de Versailles
Jules Hardouin-Mansart
Orangery, 1684–1686

ABOVE:
south façade
FACING PAGE:
view of south-west corner

New Splendour and New Developments

The Orangery at Versailles was the admiration of all who saw it, even before Hardouin-Mansart's work was complete. Working with Le Nôtre, he reproduced the same design in 1682 at Chantilly for the Grand Condé. Two years later, at the Château of Sceaux, he created a new design for the son of Colbert, the Marquis de Seignelay. The orangery, to one side of the main château courtyard, was a large building, some 80 m (265 ft) in length (until during the war of 1870 one end was destroyed); it had a raised roof and pediments decorated with ornate reliefs. In summer it was also used for musical performances and other entertainments.

The new role of the orangery as a place of entertainment was less common in France than in the German principalities, but was true of Saint-Cloud, where the orangery was completed in 1688 by Jean Girard. Monsieur, the brother of Louis XIV, commissioned Jacques Rousseau to provide the decor and embellish the building. Rousseau was highly regarded for his skill in creating an illusion of distance through the use of *trompe l'œil* perspective. At Saint-Cloud he transformed the long gallery into a charming garden room in which the Duchess of Orléans could hold banquets *al fresco* when the weather was overcast.

The orange tree itself, like the orangery, became subject to all manner of strategies designed to lessen its austere appearance and the severity of the formal beds. In his gardens at Clagny the Marquis de Montespan invented a device which delighted Mme de Sévigné: "There is a small grove of orange trees grown in large containers; they form avenues of shade in which one can walk at ease; to conceal the containers there are fences on each side at elbow height covered with climbers, roses, jasmine, and carnations; it is without doubt the most beautiful, remarkable, and charming novelty that one could imagine and I am truly fond of it".

Château de Sceaux
Ile-de-France
Jules Hardouin-Mansart
Orangery, 1684

ABOVE:
view of south-east corner
FACING PAGE BELOW:
view of south-west corner

LEFT:
Château de Fontainebleau
Ile-de-France
Garden of Diana
orange tree beds, c. 1680
engraving by Nicolas de Poilly

LEFT:
Château de Chantilly
Ile-de-France
Jules Hardouin-Mansart
and André Le Nôtre
Orangery and formal beds, 1682–1686
engraving by Nicolas de Poilly

LEFT AND FACING PAGE BELOW:
Wilhelm Friedrich Isenflamm,
Baron von Gleichen-Russwurm
**Observations
microscopiques...**, 1770
Floral allegories

Château de Sceaux
Ile-de-France
Jules Hardouin-Mansart
Orangery, 1684
pediment details

<small>ABOVE:</small>
Summer
<small>FACING PAGE BELOW:</small>
Autumn

Château de Vendeuvre
Normandy
Orangery, 1785

RIGHT AND FACING PAGE BELOW:
ornamental figures on the façade
FACING PAGE ABOVE:
south-west façade

LEFT:
Château de Cheverny
Val de Loire
Orangery, c. 1764
south façade

The Orangery –
a New Identity

The orangery began to appear in architectural treatises at the end of the seventeenth century and in a work published in 1737, *De la distribution des maisons de plaisance*, an entire chapter was devoted to it by the author, Jacques-François Blondel, director of the Ecole des Arts. Such recognition did not, however, confer any real autonomy on the building as it was treated simply as a lateral extension of the main building, the other wing housing the kitchens and pantries. Until the second half of the eighteenth century the siting of the orangery would continue to be conditioned by a single imperative: that any enhancement of the orangery remain subject to the harmony of the composition as a whole.

However, the orangery on the Cheverny estate (in the Sologne area of Blois) is seventeenth century in style, like the château, but stands on its own to the north of the château on the "garden side". This highly unusual arrangement appears quite out of keeping with the rules current at the time. The château, which was rebuilt between 1625 and 1632 for Henri Hurault, governor and bailiff of Blois, was acquired in 1764 by the writer of memoirs Jean-Nicolas Dufort de Saint-Léon, who immediately began major refurbishment works based on plans for the modernization of the château dating from the previous century. The orangery became part of this development and provided an ideal opportunity to echo the château's front façade. Like the château it was built in a highly classical style and embellished, but situated at a distance from the existing quadrangle. It also provided a finishing point and highlight to the grounds adjoining the rear façade, still in shade.

In Normandy, on the other hand, at the châteaux of Bény-sur-mer and Vendeuvre, the orangery forms an integral and customary part of the overall composition. The orangery at Bény-sur-mer, constructed by Monsieur de Bernières shortly before the grounds were laid out in 1745, provides a pleasant termination to the side vista from the château terrace. And the pavilion and gallery in the Italian style give the kitchen and fruit gardens the charm of a "secret garden".

At the château owned by Jacques-Alexandre Le Forestier, Comte de Vendeuvre, the normal hierarchy was more rigorously observed. The orangery was built in 1785 to match the stables, with vaulted ceilings and a warm-air ducting system to meet its functional requirements. Today it has been converted into a charming museum but still remains an excellent example of the work of Jacques-François Blondel: an elegant country house approached via extensive formal grounds.

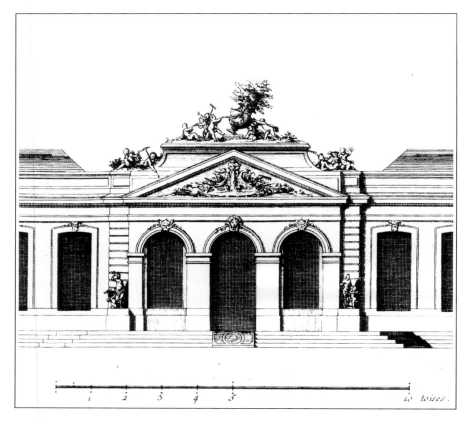

Château de Louvigny
Normandy
Orangery, c. 1760
south façade detail

FACING PAGE:
Château de Bény-sur-Mer
Normandy
Orangery, c. 1740
pavilion and gallery "in the Italian style"

LEFT:
Jacques-François Blondel
**De la distribution des
maisons de plaisance,** 1737
elevation of Orangery façade

2

NEW DIRECTIONS

From indoor garden to pleasure dome

"The garden has a theatrical role to play, providing the city dweller with a new identity."[1] The garden's new role was to provide a poetic reinterpretation of nature, an environment in which the city dweller could don any mask he chose; it was a development that would be long-lived. From the Renaissance onwards the art of garden design, like set design, underwent major changes, with theatrical and garden designers developing similar techniques for the manipulation of reality. Architects adopted the perspective techniques used for theatrical sets to enhance the illusion of space in their garden plans while set designers were quick to borrow fantastical garden features, such as grottos, fountains, and sacred groves. The sets designed for ballets and opera-ballets were full of mountains that opened up, grottos of fantastical animals, and fountains that sprang forth when conjured by a Circe or Armide.[2]

In May 1664 the young Louis XIV, wishing to dazzle his entourage, chose the gardens of Versailles, still under construction at the time, as the setting for an event known as *Plaisirs de l'Ile enchantée*. This consisted of three days of celebrations with games, banquets, and balls, and the ornamental ponds were illuminated to provide an enchanting set for a comedy-ballet by Lully and Molière: *La Princesse d'Elide*. The main purpose of the spectacle was to dazzle royalty from other parts of Europe and establish the overwhelming supremacy of the French court.

Nothing could now eclipse Louis XIV, the Sun King, and when André Campra created his opera-ballet *L'Europe galante* in 1697, the eyes of all the courts of Europe, and those of Germany in particular, turned towards Versailles and sought to imitate its splendour. Princes from across the Rhine took the magnificent gardens at Versailles as a model for a new style of living. Their royal residences had remained feudal in appearance with fortifications and a cumbersome keep surrounded by a deep moat. And the gardens, which were separated from the castle by this enclosure, were themselves still enclosed and divided up in a very traditional manner. The main interest of those who owned the Empire's many bishoprics, duchies, landgravates, and margravates was, when the persistent wars allowed, the abundance of their game and the excellence of their wines. The taste for fine gardens and rare plants was shared only by the rich bourgeoisie, who cultivated priceless fruit trees, such as the sweet orange, and precious flowers, such as the tulip, hyacinth, and Persian iris, in the grounds of their opulent town houses.

There were, however, exceptions among the members of foreign royal families. Frederick V, the Elector Palatine, was one, commissioning Salomon de Caus, a French engineer and physician, to design the remarkable new gardens for his Heidelberg residence. De Caus, who was professor of art at the English court, left London for the Palatinate in 1613 in the service of Elizabeth Stuart, daughter of James I and the Elector's young wife. He took as his inspiration the spacious design of the gardens at the Villa d'Este at Tivoli and extended the royal gardens down to the banks of the river Neckar. He incorporated "every possible unusual feature", such as grottos with surprise water features and "moving" fountains.[3]

Although the "unusual features" Salomon de Caus used were not original he was, however, the first to design an orangery that would continue to serve as a model into the next century. This was no longer a removable structure or a building half-concealed below a terrace; his was a design that not only met the requirements of these tender plants, with its tall glazed panels, even on the roof, but also demonstrated some research into form and ornamentation. This could be seen in the façade, which was punctuated by double columns in a "pastoral" style – the shaft being "in imitation of a tree trunk, with bark and knots" – and the roof concealed by a cornice with balustrade and ornamental vases. These features reflect the architect's concern for the aesthetics of a building which until that time had always been treated from a purely utilitarian point of view.

Though de Caus was a precursor of future developments he was not, unfortunately, in the vanguard as the orangery he designed was never constructed and the gardens at Heidelberg no longer exist.[4] In 1688 Louis XIV claimed the Palatinate for his sister-in-law Elisabeth Charlotte, sole heir of the von der Pfalz family, and permitted his troops, under the command of Louvois, to burn towns and countryside in the region. This order was so efficiently executed that part of the royal residence and all its grounds disappeared into the river Neckar along with the ruins of Heidelberg.

At the end of the century the courts of Germany (with the exception of the Lower Palatinate), from that of the Emperor to those of many minor noblemen, finally saw the end of fifty terrible years that followed the signature, in 1648, of the Treaty of Westphalia which had put an end to the Thirty Years War. In 1793 Schiller wrote, "Fields stood empty and infertile, palaces destroyed by fire, the countryside laid waste, and villages reduced to ashes, presenting a scene of appalling devastation".[5]

Germany had been bled dry, having lost nearly half its population, and now found itself dangerously fragmented. The Emperor, Ferdinand III, emerged from this with his power severely diminished, whereas the three hundred or so free principalities and towns saw their independence strengthened. The prime concern of every church dignitary and minor royal, whose power was now virtually absolute, was to restore life to the fields laid waste, revitalize the economic activity of the state, and rebuild the palaces and towns. There were many, like the Great Elector in Berlin and the Margrave of Brandenburg-Bayreuth at Erlangen, who welcomed the arrival of Huguenot immigrants who repopulated the villages and, most importantly, set up new industries that were soon flourishing.[6] This new opulence brought with it a grandiose, and often single, preoccupation: each principality wanted to boast a court as magnificent as that of France – Versailles remained the standard by which all other courts were judged.

Rebuilding work began at the end of the seventeenth century supervised by French specialists and garden architects in particular. In Vienna, some years after the Emperor, Leopold I, had commissioned Fischer von Erlach to draw up plans for the Schönbrunn that would eclipse Versailles, Jean Trehet was called in to create a garden in the French style adjoining the residence. In Berlin Sophie Charlotte, the charming wife of the Elector of Brandenburg – later to become Frederick I of Prussia – asked her cousin, Elisabeth Charlotte, the famous princess palatine and sister-in-law of Louis XIV, to send her Siméon Godeau, a pupil of Le Nôtre, to design the gardens of the new palace. It was also Elisabeth Charlotte who advised her aunt and faithful correspondent, the Duchess of Hanover, to engage Martin Charbonnier to create the Herrenhausen gardens in 1696.[7]

This craving for prestige continued to grow during the following century. "Life in the German courts was to blossom, if not as brilliantly as in other places, certainly with greater freedom than elsewhere".[8] Princes and prelates, avid for new sensations, expected all the artists in their employ – architects, painters, stucco artists, master-gardeners, and also directors of ballet and masters of ceremony – to exercise their talents to transform palace life into a never-ending entertainment. This frenzied quest produced a flurry of new

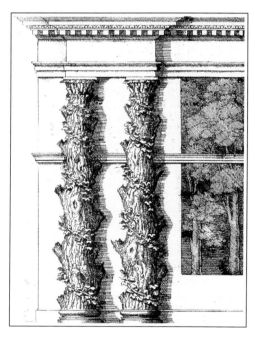

Salomon de Caus
Hortus palatinus, 1620
*Design for the orangery in the gardens of
the Elector Palatine, Heidelberg* (detail)

summer residences, the so-called *Lusthäuser*. The names these residences were given – La Solitude, La Favorite, L'Ermitage, Sans-Pareil, and Sans-Souci – show that the German principalities no longer had any reason to envy France, having adopted the language, customs, entertainments, and, of course, the artists of that country, some of whom had in fact become resident in Germany. Some artists remained in the employ of a single prince for the whole of their career. The Landgrave of Hesse-Kassel engaged the services of Paul du Ry (a pupil of Nicolas-François Blondel) and then of Louis Rémy de La Fosse, who was later, in 1714, appointed architect-in-chief of the principality of Hesse-Darmstadt. In 1743 Carl Eugen, Duke of Württemberg, engaged Pierre-Louis-Philippe de La Guépière, and in 1745 Joseph Saint-Pierre became permanently attached to the court of the Margravine of Bayreuth, while Nicolas de Pigage, from Lorraine, joined the court of the Elector Palatine, Carl Theodor, in 1749.[9]

In fact it was this fascination with appearance and theatricality, rather than the refinement and elegance of certain architectural designs, that allowed the French spirit to blossom and come into its own. It could be found in the residences' rooms with their pastel panelling highlighted with gold and in the outdoor auditoriums where the great repertoire of France vied with the opera of Italy. The most acclaimed actors were those from Paris and at Mannheim Carl Theodor, the Elector Palatine, kept a troupe of French players for almost twenty years. In Berlin the French actor Henri Louis Lekain received ovations for his interpretations of the great roles of Oedipus, Mahomet, and Orosmane in the tragedies of Voltaire, and the pretty French dancer Babette Cochois delighted the court with her impish grace. At Ansbach the principality's last margrave became captivated by Mademoiselle Clairon, a member of the Comédie Française.[10]

"A prince might behave as foolishly as he pleased if this amused him more than plain and ordinary common sense which, after all, was the province of the bourgeoisie. It is therefore unsurprising to find that entertainment played a central role in the life of the German courts."[11] In its attempts to satisfy the unbridled ambitions of its monarch one court surpassed all others – this was the court of Saxony under Frederick Augustus I, better known as Augustus the Strong.

In 1694, to captivate the young Swedish countess, Maria Aurora de Königsmark, who was his first love, Frederick Augustus (who, legend has it, went on to have almost seven hundred mistresses) created the most voluptuous of settings. We are told by Baron Karl Ludwig von Pöllnitz, writing twenty years later, that "the performance took place on an island on which stood a tent furnished in the Turkish style. There guests were greeted by two young Orientals offering refreshments. Then the 'Great Master' appeared amidst the officers of the seraglio. This was the Elector himself, who took his seat on a sofa beside Aurora. Oriental dances were performed and the prince led Aurora to a gondola and took his place beside her ..."[12]

In Germany, more than elsewhere, the vast gardens of the residences played an essential role in the variety of spectacles that were held – displays, dances, masked balls, and promenades with a mythological theme, each ending with a magnificent firework display. At first sight they appeared to represent an ideal world, a world immutably ordered, "a world without conflict or discord",[13] governed by an etiquette as strictly laid out as the endless lines of avenues and neatly trimmed arbours. In fact the gardens reflected the twin natures of their owners: beyond the splendid excesses of the esplanades and formal gardens features of a more informal nature could be found – pavilions for bathing, music, or banqueting, tea pavilions or *Kaffeehäuser*, outdoor theatres or aviaries in a variety of styles, situated at the intersections of avenues under the protection of trelliswork arbours, or in wooded groves – these were the real raison d'être of the gardens.

In Germany the orangery occupied a special and unique place in the entertainment of the royal courts, not afforded it by any other nation. During the first half of the eighteenth century German princes and prelates assigned it a new role, seeking to satisfy their predilection for artifice through the opulence and decor of these buildings. They had no more desire to commune with nature in their orangeries than they had in their gardens: the gods and goddesses who peopled their groves and gardens and decorated the walls and ceilings of their residences were there to allow them to "immerse themselves in the sense of their own sublimity".[14]

The role played by the orangery in the life of the court resulted in it becoming an integral part of the palace itself, particularly during the first decades of the eighteenth century. At Charlottenburg in 1709, and at Nymphenburg in 1716, the architects Johann Friedrich Eosander and Josef Effner found the orangery provided the ideal solution to extending the reception rooms of the residences. To emphasize its palatial nature the orangery needed to be treated with the same grandeur of style as the rest of the residence but also in keeping with the overall design and characteristics of the existing building.

This was an ambitious plan that led architects to interrupt the customary long gallery used for the storage of orange trees with a higher central section housing a *Gartensaal*.[15] This "garden room" was decorated with stucco or *trompe l'œil* work and intentionally constructed on two levels in the Italian style, with a promenade gallery overlooking the room below. It was ideal for festivities that extended onto the terrace, offering an advantage that the ceremonial rooms on the principal floor of the residence could not, and thus became a distinctive feature of many orangeries built in Germany. From the outset guests were enthralled by their splendour. "The celebrations took place in the orangery adjoining the palace. When I went in," recounts the young French painter and interior designer Joseph Binet, "all the guests were assembled. In the light of the many torches and Venetian lanterns a curious spectacle presented itself to me. The long room was filled with oriental hangings and rugs, transparent drapes and brocades among which sparkled splendid jewels, creating a scene that could well have graced the set of the tale of the Arabian Nights in a Paris theatre".[16]

The "garden room" became increasingly imposing and gradually supplanted the orangery's original purpose and its relationship with the gardens. At Fulda in 1722 the architect Maximilian von Welsch created a building of such splendour, dominating the grounds from the top of a monumental staircase and crowned by a pediment bearing the royal coat of arms, that it completely masked the two side wings used for orange trees.

At Dresden, the capital of Saxony, the same development took place – the orangery became a venue for festivities and performances – but in this case with a degree of splendour that was quite unprecedented. As we have seen, even before he began to enlarge his ancestors' austere residence, the celebrated Elector, Frederick Augustus, had aspired to bring a new brilliance to his court and in 1709 commissioned his architect, Matthäus Daniel Pöppelmann, to build a Royal Orangery.

The site set aside for the new orangery demonstrates clearly the real purpose for which it was built. To the south-west of the palace a large area had been cleared during the construction of the new city walls in 1574. It was here that some temporary buildings for court entertainments had been constructed – a theatre, and rooms for celebrations and tournaments – with the *Zwingergarten* or Fortress Garden to one side. Again in 1709, Frederick Augustus had ordered the construction of a wooden amphitheatre not far from here in which parades to celebrate the recovery of his title of King of Poland and the arrival of his cousin Frederick IV of Denmark could be held. Once these festivities were over Pöppelmann, who was still taken by the concept, decided to give the new orangery a double purpose: it was to provide both an Italian-style decor and a magnificent auditorium for a vast theatrical set. From the "Rampart" pavilion in the background concealed stairs lead to a roof garden planted with orange trees. Extending out in a horseshoe to each side are two long gallery-loggias whose flat roofs also serve as wide balcony promenades. Each wing terminates in another pavilion, the

Grotto Pavilion and the Marble Pavilion opening on to the marvellous Pool of the Nymphs. However, the Royal Orangery would not reach its final size or truly fulfil its magnificent new role until 1719, when Pöppelmann matched it with an identical structure on the city side of the residence.

The architect went on to design extensive new gardens leading from the grounds of the Orangery, or Zwinger as it was already known, to a new royal residence overlooking the river Elbe. But the Prince had developed new interests such as the Japanese Palace or Pillnitz residence. Pöppelmann had to content himself with completing the work already undertaken and in 1728 the Elector held a final celebration there in honour of the King of Prussia, Frederick William I, and of the *Kronprinz*, later to become Frederick the Great. Sixteen years later the young King began work on his new residence at Potsdam, the palace of Sans-Souci.[17]

The orangery built by Frederick Augustus, though soon abandoned, remained unrivalled in Germany. No other orangery would aim to fulfil its combined role of stage, auditorium, and set. Nevertheless, for many architects this remained a key element in garden design.

In some instances, as at Erlangen, the orangery was built on a slight curve, framing the formal beds, and was connected to the palace by an open gallery. More spectacularly, it marks the vanishing point of the whole composition extending behind the palace, the site being determined by the situation to the north of the garden-side façade of the palace. The position of the orangery opposite the palace not only gives it the best orientation but also transforms it into a mirror reflecting the palace in the sunlight just as effectively as those framed in the gilded panelling of the rooms. A plan with such dramatic potential was naturally adopted in many royal gardens: at Gaibach, the family residence of Prince-Bishop Lothar Franz von Schönborn, as early as 1700; at Weikersheim in 1719 for the young wife of Count Karl Ludwig von Hohenlohe; and at Wiesbaden in 1721 for Prince George Augustus von Nassau-Idstein.[18]

The orangery, constructed in a wide variety of styles – rectilinear, horseshoe-shaped, and semicircular – soon began to determine the overall layout of the other buildings and alone decided the design of the formal beds and wooded areas. For some princes, still under the influence of a *Kavalierstour* in which they had succumbed to the charms of Italy, the orangery became a symbol of a rediscovered Arcadia, particularly in winter. On estates such as Karlsaue near Kassel, and Schwetzingen near Heidelberg, the orangery with its dominant position, extensions, and many uses, in fact became the principal royal residence. Paradoxically, this prestigious new role meant that the orangery became less and less indispensable. It had now developed many forms – the palatial orangery with a raised roof, the long, scenic galleries of the orangery as decor, and the orangery-residence with its Italianate terraces – but all had become so closely identified with the country house that, when the Ermitage palace near Bayreuth and the Sans-Souci residence at Potsdam were built, they in fact adopted the formal characteristics of the orangery, its proportions, layout and decor.

After holding centre stage for many years the royal orangery began to disappear and by the 1750s was being replaced by more "rational" buildings, functional orangeries built at the order of enlightened princes whose pleasures were not to be found in balls and masquerades.

The spirit of the Enlightenment was spreading; in Dresden the Royal Orangery had already become the Royal Palace of Science and, since 1746, the Grotto Pavilion had housed the Mathematics and Physics Hall. In 1775 Goethe revived interest in botany among the royal princes and encouraged some, the Grand Duke Charles Augustus at Weimar being one, to enlarge or convert their orangeries into hot houses to be used exclusively for their collections of rare plants.

"It was now simpler to find pleasure in meditation, poetry, and scientific study than in the incessant excitement of which each had felt compelled to be a part in order to "kill" the time he had felt unable to beguile."[19]

Theodor Zwinger
Theatrum botanicum, 1696
Frontispiece

The Orangery as Palace

The step from a palace with an orangery to an orangery of palatial proportions was but a small one. The Prince-Abbot of Fulda, Adolph von Dalberg, closely connected to the powerful religious dignitaries of the Schönborn family, was quick to perceive the advantages of a scheme which would allow him to satisfy his ambition and rival his distinguished neighbours. Naturally, he borrowed their painters, their stucco artists, and their architects.

In 1722 the Prince-Abbot instructed the superintendent of works at Mainz, Maximilian von Welsch, to construct an impressive orangery opposite the residence. This was completed in 1726 under the direction of Andreas Gallasini, the new court architect.

The building dominates the gardens with its enormous, monumental staircase, its palatial appearance revealing nothing of its original purpose. However, a towering vase – the work of the sculptor Daniel Friedrich Humbach – serves as a reminder of the original function of the orangery. And yet, no sooner is the threshold of the tall French windows crossed than confusion again reigns supreme. The ornate walls of the interior are in the Italian style, stucco pilasters framing the tall openings and loggias, and are extended upwards by a fantastical colonnade, a *trompe l'œil* extravaganza by the court painter Emmanuel Wohlhaupter. In 1730, after a period in Italy from which he returned deeply impressed by the luminous compositions of Giambattista Piazzetta, the artist was commissioned to create the decor for the room in collaboration with the stucco artist Andreas Schwarzmann.

True to the tradition of the period the painter brings the room alive by adorning it with all the popular imagery of the time: from the balcony Ottoman princes look upon the spectacle of the gods and goddesses of the rivers and seasons fraternizing with allegories of the four continents, while, crowning it all, Apollo in his chariot transports the powerful Prince-Abbot himself.

Fulda Palace
Hessen
Maximilian von Welsch and Andreas Gallasini
Orangery, 1722–1726

Above:
pediment on the central pavilion
Left:
south façade
Facing page:
Daniel Friedrich Humbach
Flora, 1728

Fulda Palace
Hessen
Orangery, 1722–1726
Gartensaal or Apollo Room, 1730
Emmanuel Wohlhaupter
fresco

BELOW:
view from below

Fulda Palace
Hessen
Orangery, 1722–1726
Gartensaal or Apollo Room, 1730
Emmanuel Wohlhaupter
fresco

<small>Facing page above,
above and right:</small>
details

The *Gartensaal* was masterfully reinterpreted at the residences built between 1711 and 1749 for the great church dignitaries of Franconia, members of the powerful Schönborn family. The greatest architects of the period were brought in and consulted; Johann Dientzenhofer, Maximilian von Welsch, and Johann Balthasar Neumann worked on site during the building of the palaces of Bruchsal, Pommersfelden, and Würzburg. And while construction was underway, Johann Lucas von Hildebrandt, an architect at the court of Vienna, and Germain Boffrand were also called in by the prince-bishops of Bamberg and Würzburg.

In each case the architects planned a *Gartensaal* on the ground floor of the palace opening onto the gardens. Although it may have served the same function as in an orangery, the decor often recalled a nymphs' grotto or the *sala terrena* of the villas of Tuscany and Rome.

At the Bruchsal residence built for the prince-bishop of Speyer and Constance, the architect Johann Balthasar Neumann, who replaced Maximilian von Welsch in 1731, covered the "Garden Room" with a large rib-vault ceiling decorated by fresco paintings evoking the mysterious grottos of the gardens of Italy. At the Weissenstein palace at Pommersfelden, the residence of the Prince-Bishop of Bamberg, it was the famous Grotto of Theatis in the gardens at Versailles that Georg Hennicke and the stucco artist Daniel Schenk tried to emulate in 1722. They decorated the room in rocaille with a mixture of porous rock, pebbles, shells, and crystals framing floral and grotesque motifs. Thin strips of mica set among coloured stucco sparkle in the light from the high windows and give the illusion of a fine mosaic of molten glass.

In 1749 Johann Balthasar Neumann completed work on the Prince-Bishop's residence at Würzburg and Antonio Bossi decorated the *Gartensaal* with white stuccowork. The wide gallery that runs round the room appears to give onto a mysterious garden, but in fact looks onto the vast *trompe l'œil* work by Johann Zick depicting the *Feast of the Gods* and *Diana at Rest*.

ABOVE:
Maximilian von Welsch and Johann Balthasar Neumann
Bruchsal Residence, 1722–1732
Baden-Württemberg
Gartensaal, 1732

LEFT:
Theatrum Europaeum, c. 1750
*Perspective view of the Main Hall
in the centre of the Orangery at Charlottenburg*

FACING PAGE:
Johann Balthasar Neumann, Johann Dientzenhofer and Maximilian von Welsch
Würzburg Residence, 1720–1749
Bavaria
Gartensaal, 1749–1750

Profpect des Sallons in der mitten von der Orangerie zu Charlottenburg

Weissenstein Palace, Pommersfelden
Bavaria
Georg Hennicke, rocaille ornamentation,
and Daniel Schenk, stuccowork
Sala Terrena, 1722–1723

ABOVE AND FACING PAGE BELOW:
transverse views

**Weissenstein Palace,
Pommersfelden**
Bavaria
Georg Hennicke, rocaille
ornamentation, and
Daniel Schenk, stuccowork
Sala Terrena, 1722–1723

Right and
facing page below:
vault details

The Orangery as Royal Theatre

In 1729, to celebrate the completion of work on the Royal Orangery at Dresden, Matthäus Daniel Pöppelmann published a magnificent work entitled *Vorstellung und Beschreibung des ... erbauten sogenannten Zwingergartens.* The work also honoured his royal client the Prince-Elector of Saxony and King of Poland.

Before succeeding his father in 1694, the young Frederick Augustus had travelled in France and Italy in the company of the architect Wolf Caspar von Klengel. He was deeply impressed by Hardouin-Mansart's work at Versailles and once back in Dresden asked the court architect Christoph Beyer to draw up plans for an orangery, based on a pencil sketch he himself had made. This project, set aside during the War of the Spanish Succession, was taken up again in 1709, under the direction of Pöppelmann, a young architect from Westphalia.

In 1710, after the first plans had been drawn up, the Elector again intervened, sending his architect to Prague, Vienna, and Rome to consult the most celebrated architects of the period.

Pöppelmann, however, became even more interested in the stately residences of the Roman countryside. Back in Dresden Pöppelmann worked in collaboration with the sculptor Balthasar Permoser, who had been appointed to the court of Saxony after working in Italy to re-create the ornamental profusion displayed in the gardens of these villas. Together the architect and the sculptor worked to achieve a perfect synthesis between architecture and plastic orna-mentation, to the point where their respective roles appeared to be reversed. The terms on the central pavilion and the satyrs on the galleries become load-bearing elements while the blind arcades and columns are reduced to no more than decorative features.

Matthäus Daniel Pöppelmann
The Zwinger or Royal Orangery, 1709–1728
Dresden, Saxony
Rampart Pavilion, 1711–1713
Balthasar Permoser and studio
sculptures

Above and facing page below:
Hermes on north-west façade

Matthäus Daniel Pöppelmann
The Zwinger or Royal Orangery, 1709–1728
Dresden, Saxony
Rampart Pavilion, 1711–1713
Balthasar Permoser and studio
sculptures

<small>Left and facing page below:</small>
Atlantes on south-east façade

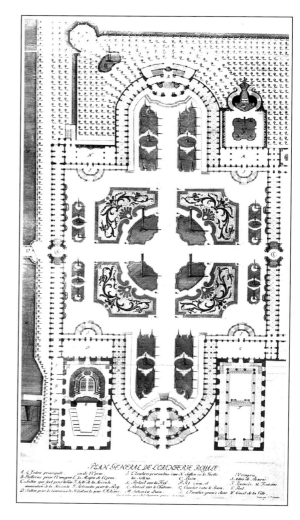

Matthäus Daniel Pöppelmann
The Zwinger or Royal Orangery, 1709–1728
Dresden, Saxony

Matthäus Daniel Pöppelmann
**Vorstellung und Beschreibung des ...
erbauten sogenannten Zwingergartens,** 1729
Frontispiece

Matthäus Daniel Pöppelmann
The Zwinger or Royal Orangery, 1709–1728
Dresden, Saxony
Nymphs' Pool, 1713–1714

LEFT, BELOW AND FACING PAGE
ABOVE LEFT AND BELOW:
Balthasar Permoser and studio
Nymphs, 1715–1718

Antonio Porta and Gottfried von Gedeler
Erlangen Palace, 1700–1704
Bavaria
Gottfried von Gedeler
Orangery, 1705–1706

RIGHT:
west façade on the palace side
BELOW AND FACING PAGE ABOVE:
Elias Räntz, pediment details

The Orangery as Stage Set

The orangeries built by the lesser dignitaries, the margraves, although not as splendid as those of the more powerful prince-electors, were more than utilitarian constructions and played a key role in achieving the theatrical effect desired in garden design of the period.

In some cases, as at Erlangen, a small town in the margravate of Brandenburg-Bayreuth, the orangery stands opposite the main residence. In 1703 Prince Christian Ernst presented this new residence, on which construction had begun three years earlier, to his third wife, the young Elisabeth Sophie, one of the three daughters of Frederick I of Prussia. In 1705, at the request of the Margravine, the Berlin architect Gottfried von Gedeler completed the composition of the gardens with an orangery and an identical pavilion to be used as a reception room, both curving inwards on each side of the main residence, echoing the arabesque lines of the formal beds. In the fashion of the time the architect placed the orange garden behind the orangery so that the orangery itself would appear to be ornamental rather than functional. He accentuated this effect by decorating the pediments with allegories of the four seasons.

At the Weikersheim Palace, for another young princess, Elisabeth Frederika Sophia von Oettingen, the architect Johann Christian Lüttich used the orangery as a key element in a vast dramatic garden composition. The elegant orangery provides a "backdrop", while the gardens themselves, laid out by Daniel Matthieu in 1708, become the "stalls" in which the gods of the winds and the goddesses of the seasons take their places and the great rooms on the principal floor of the palace are transformed into "royal boxes" for the court.

Constructed as two separate halves the orangery draws the gaze out over the countryside and the valley of the Tauber towards the distant horizon. Still on the theme of Italian theatre Lüttich finishes the orangery buildings with a colonnade and exedra, at a slight distance from the façade. Those ever-present players, the gods of Olympus, sculpted by the studio of Johann Jakob Sommer, dominate the whole, seated on the balustrades of the cornices or emerging from their niches as from the wings of a theatre.

RIGHT:
Erlangen Palace, 1700–1704
Bavaria
Perspective view of the palace and gardens
etching after Paul Decker, c. 1710

Weikersheim Palace
Baden-Württemberg
Daniel Matthieu
Gardens, 1708
Johann Christian Lüttich
Orangery, 1719–1723

<small>ABOVE:</small>
colonnade with exedra, detail
<small>FACING PAGE:</small>
general view

<small>LEFT:</small>
Johann Bernhard Fischer von Erlach
Entwurf einer historischen Architektur, 1725
*Roman vase and pavilions at the
entrance to the garden*

The Orangery as Residence

For a court that was both free-thinking and open-minded the orangery often provided a more suitable environment than the royal residence. These princes wanted the orangery to be distinct from the palace and, in many cases, for it to be so splendid as to outshine the royal residence itself. As a result of this it was the orangery that now became the deciding feature in the way gardens were laid out and, as at Kassel and Schwetzingen, even dictated the overall design.

By 1703 the Italian architect Giovanni Francesco Guerniero had worked at Kassel for two years on a huge cascade tumbling down the Karlsberg for the gardens of Wilhelmshöhe, but the Landgrave, Karl von Hesse-Kassel, abandoned the project as too large and costly; by 1718 only one third of the work had been completed. Now weary of theatricality the Landgrave appointed the French architect Paul du Ry, who had arrived at the court following the revocation of the Edict of Nantes, and the master gardener Johann Adam Wunsdorf to design the new estate of Karlsaue. The Prince decided that the residence must be built in the style of an immense orangery: it was designed as a bright, airy loggia, entirely dominating the design of the gardens, divided by three main radiating avenues, and the whole composition surrounded by a canal magnificently designed in the shape of a viola da gamba. During the course of the work du Ry collaborated with Rémy de La Fosse.

To complement the gardens designed by Wunsdorf, the master gardener, the two architects created a delightful building with a roof in the Italian style, an elegant façade with curved pediments decorated with reliefs of Roman inspiration. Only the two-tone finish in lemon and eggshell reflected local taste.

The interior arrangements demonstrate a concern for comfort that was still unusual at that period. To ensure that the two wings would continue to provide a pleasant promenade during the long winter months the galleries were heated by underfloor air ducts fed with warm air by an ingenious blower system. The Dutch were already experimenting with a system of this kind but it was the presence at the court of the French physician Denis Papin, who had been protected and supported by the Landgrave since 1687, that enabled the technique to be applied to a building of such proportions. Between 1722 and 1765 the orangery was further enhanced by the addition of a Kitchen Pavilion and a Bath Pavilion, paved and finished in marble.

Karlsaue Residence
Kassel, Hessen
Paul du Ry and Rémy de La Fosse
Orangery, 1703–1711

FACING PAGE ABOVE:
entrance to the left wing
LEFT AND FACING PAGE BELOW:
pediment details
BELOW:
general view

At Schwetzingen the orangery was again transformed into a royal residence but here its new role was dictated entirely by the Prince, who was passionate about music and theatre.

In 1748, to convert the family hunting lodge near Heidelberg, Carl Theodor, the Elector Palatine, turned not to one of his court architects, but to the famous theatrical designer Alessandro Galli da Bibiena. Bibiena's design consisted of two curving galleries – an orangery and a reception room – built on either side of the pavilion, and alongside a formal bed from which all the avenues of the garden would radiate out. These galleries, with adjoining trellis-work arbours, would provide a "set" of immense proportions framing the vast esplanade designed by Johann Ludwig Petri. The ornamental pool at the centre of this design was reserved for the poet Arion, rescued from the water by Apollo, reflecting the Prince's belief that only the arts could ensure Man's survival.

Nicolas de Pigage, who took over from Galli da Bibiena in 1749, provided the project with the finishing touches worthy of a royal residence. One of the most important requirements was to provide an extended set for the performances taking place in the charming theatre constructed in 1752 behind one of the wings. A troupe of French actors attached to the court gave an inaugural performance there in 1753 of *Zaïre* by Voltaire, who was a guest of the Elector that year.

The two wings of the orangery, completed in 1754, fulfilled their new function so successfully that the orangery's original role was soon forgotten. In fact when the Elector developed an interest in exotic plants Nicolas de Pigage was obliged to build a second orangery to house them. The new building, which was started in 1762, had an adjoining garden, divided by small channels in the Arab style, and with wide lawns and avenues of fine sand adorned by hundreds of container-grown orange, lemon, palm, and banana trees. Nevertheless, the architect felt compelled to recall the primary purpose for which the Schwetzingen palace had been built and transformed this magnificent garden into an open-air antechamber and extension of the outdoor theatre completed the following year.

Schwetzingen Palace
Baden-Württemberg
Orangery, 1748–1754

ABOVE:
Nicolas de Pigage
orange tree wing, 1754
FACING PAGE:
Alessandro Galli da Bibiena and Nicolas de Pigage
reception room wing, 1748–1749
LEFT:
Johann Ludwig Petri
circular bed, 1753
Barthélemy Guibal
fountain of Arion

Schwetzingen Palace
Baden-Württemberg
Nicolas de Pigage
New Orangery, 1762–1763

ABOVE:
front view
FACING PAGE BELOW:
transverse view

RIGHT:
Johann Anton Glantschnigg
allegory of Europe and Asia, c. 1745

Variations on the Orangery

From the middle of the eighteenth century architects attempted to reverse a process that had now become common. Having transformed the orangery into a place of residence they now set about applying the typical features of the orangery to create a new style of country house.

This assimilation of style found its finest expression in two small residences built at the same period for Princess Wilhelmina of Brandenburg-Bayreuth and her brother King Frederick II of Prussia.

At Bayreuth the margravine took great pleasure in performing as an actress and musician and was also a keen writer. This was her way of forgetting the unhappy years of her youth spent in Berlin; her brutal and despotic father, Frederick William I of Prussia, a monarch of military inclination (he was known as the "Sergeant-King") had dismissed all the artists and performers at Charlottenburg and had converted the palace into a barracks.

Under the influence of this young woman the somewhat gloomy court of Bayreuth was to become one of the most brilliant in Europe. In 1747, the court architect, Joseph Saint-Pierre, completed the Sans Pareil park with its allegorical theme, he completed the Opera, and in 1749 was commissioned to build a new palace at L'Ermitage, the margraves' summer residence.

The architect created a delightful palace in the style of an orangery. To lighten the effect he extended the façade with an arcade, giving the two curving wings the appearance of an open loggia. The new residence, decorated by the stucco artist Giovanni Battista with a mosaic of stone that sparkled in the sunlight, was like the setting for a pastorale, as ethereal as its reflection in the large ornamental pool that replaced the customary formal garden.

In Berlin Frederick II of Prussia also adopted a theatrical theme for the design of the new Sans Souci Palace. However, unlike his sister

Bayreuth Palace
Bavaria
Joseph Saint-Pierre
New Hermitage Palace, 1749–1753
Marble facework by Giovanni Bathista Pedrozzi

ABOVE:
Apollo Pavilion and arcades
FACING PAGE:
general view

RIGHT:
Johann Bernard Fischer von Erlach
Entwurf einer historischen Architektur, 1725
Greek vases and design for a country house

Wilhelmina, the king did not need inspiration for a new style of decor. His ambition was to recreate a Garden of the Hesperides in the north, filled with all the pleasures of both mind and senses that had delighted the ancient Greeks. In 1744 he chose his site – a large stretch of land descending gently towards the gates of the city of Potsdam. The town, which had been the summer residence of the court since 1648, had already, according to Voltaire, been transformed into a "radiant Athens". Peace reigned and Prussia was on its way to becoming a formidable power, with Austria vanquished and Silesia annexed.

Everyone wanted to change the garrison-town appearance imposed on Potsdam under Frederick William. The King had eliminated all the buildings he considered frivolous, starting with the orangery at the palace. This had been built in 1695 by Johann Arnold Nering, the architect responsible for the Lietzenburg Palace, later known as Charlottenburg, and was converted into stables in 1713. It would continue in this role but was given a new, more stylish appearance during restoration in 1746 by the architect Georg Wenzeslaus von Knobelsdorff, a favourite of Frederick II.

When work began on Sans Souci in 1744 the King asked his architect, whom he had just appointed superintendent of the palaces and gardens of Prussia, to ensure that every element of the composition was a harmonious contribution to this Arcadia for which he yearned. The single-storey residence was created in the style of an orangery with a succession of tall windows overlooking the terrace. On the façade bacchants and fauns entwined with vines – caryatids and atlantes by Friedrich Christian Glume – rise out of the stonework, gazing out over and heralding the King's vineyard rising on the terracing beyond. On the fine sandy soil of the six curving terraces hundreds of orange and lemon trees stand in neat rows, while against the supporting walls grow vines and figs, and also espalier peaches, cherries, and apricots, protected by cold frames. And to complete this garden of delights on each side of the palace but lower in height, the architect built a genuine orangery, converted in 1774 by Georg Christian Unger into guest apartments, and a hot house, replaced in 1755 by the Picture Gallery.

Sans-Souci Park
Potsdam, Brandenburg
Georg Wenzeslaus von Knobelsdorff
Orangery, 1747
conversion to guest apartments, 1774

Above:
ornamentation above the central pavilion

Sans-Souci Park
Potsdam, Brandenburg
Georg Wenzeslaus von Knobelsdorff
Orangery, 1747
conversion to guest apartments, 1774

LEFT AND FACING PAGE BELOW:
Friedrich Christian Glume
keystones with decorative heads
BELOW:
transverse view

Sans-Souci Park
Potsdam, Brandenburg
Johann Arnold Nering
Former Orangery at the Residence, 1695
Georg Wenzeslaus von Knobelsdorff
Renovation of the façade following conversion to Royal Stables, 1746

LEFT, BELOW AND FACING PAGE ABOVE:
Friedrich Christian Glume
horsemen on the cornice

Sans-Souci Park
Potsdam, Brandenburg
Johann Arnold Nering
Former Orangery at the Residence, 1695
Georg Wenzeslaus von Knobelsdorff
Renovation of the façade following conversion to Royal Stables, 1746

RIGHT:
transverse view

Georg Wenzeslaus von Knobelsdorff
Sans-Souci Palace, 1745–1747
Potsdam, Brandenburg

LEFT:
general view on the terrace side

Georg Wenzeslaus von Knobelsdorff
Sans-Souci Palace, 1745–1747
Potsdam, Brandenburg

Right, below and facing page
above:
Friedrich Christian Glume
*fauns and bacchants, atlantes and
caryatids on pillars, 1746*

Georg Wenzeslaus von Knobelsdorff
Sans-Souci Palace, 1745–1747
Potsdam, Brandenburg

<small>Facing page:</small>
general view
<small>Above:</small>
terraced vines, detail, 1744–1745

<small>Right:</small>
Johann David Schleuen
**Perspective of the King's country
house and the garden at Sans-Souci**
Engraving, c. 1760

Frederick's fascination with ancient Greece gave way to more exotic delights and in 1754 he asked the new court architect, Johann Gottfried Büring, to complete the new "Anglo-Chinese" gardens at Sans Souci with a pavilion in which tea, the fashionable new drink, could be taken.

Tea and tea-drinking were introduced into Europe in the 1630s by the Dutch East India Company. Although the Paris doctor Louis Lémery recommended it in 1702, the German courts were slower in taking it up. As late as 1712 the Princess Palatine, Elisabeth-Charlotte, is quoted as saying "I cannot bear coffee, tea, or chocolate; what I would really enjoy is a good beer soup...". These reservations were associated for a long time with a rather vague botanical understanding of the tea plant (*Camellia sinensis* or *Thea sinensis*), as demonstrated in the *Dictionnaire raisonné d'Histoire naturelle* in which it is described as related to the spindle tree and referred to as "*Evonimo affinis arbor, orientalis, flore roseo*".

On the other hand, since the shipping companies were able to "sell between eight and ten million pounds of it per year" few people were unfamiliar with the many varieties of Chinese and Japanese teas available – from Imperial tea to Courtesans' tea, brewed only from the flowers of the tea plant, and green tea, flavoured with the roots of the Florence iris.

The Chinese pavilion at Sans Souci was a product of this new fashion and although finished in 1757 was not officially opened until seven years later as the unprecedented refinement of its decor was extremely difficult to accomplish. Sheltering under a giant lily leaf musicians, princesses, and dignitaries from a fantastical Orient – sculpted life size and decorated with gold leaf by Johann Peter Benkert and Johann Matthias Gottlieb Heymüller – play on a variety of strange instruments and sample tea, melons, and pineapples from Brazil. Inside, Chinese mandarins and their favourites, privileged spectators high up in the gallery, continue the illusion of a strange new world, more imaginary than real, in which all expressions of the exotic are brought together in one place.

Sans-Souci Park
Potsdam, Brandenburg
Chinese Pavilion, 1754–1757
Johann Peter Benkert and Johann Matthias
Gottlieb Heymüller
sculptures

Facing page above:
window ornament
Above and facing page below:
oriental figures sampling
melons and pineapples
Right:
pavilion seen from the park

Sans-Souci Park
Potsdam, Brandenburg
Chinese Pavilion, 1754–1757
interior decor, 1756–1764

ABOVE AND FACING PAGE:
Thomas Huber
trompe l'œil decoration on the cupola
LEFT:
main hall

3

THE ORANGERY TRANSFORMED

The transition from the functional to the ideal

During the eighteenth century essays were published in England on the relationship between Art and Nature. The first of these, by Joseph Addison, were eventually translated into French in 1746,[1] leading to a review of "the art of creating the modern garden".[2] One result of this, as we have already seen, was a gradual decline in interest in the building of orangeries.

In England, by 1720, the determination to "embrace Nature without restraining it" had been translated into the abandonment of the customary interconnecting formal beds and avenues of fine sand ornamented by container-grown shrubs. The writings of Joseph Addison, Samuel Boyse, or William Gilpin[3] might have prompted a similar development on the Continent but in fact they made the orangery an integral part of modern garden design and an indispensable accessory in the grounds of stately homes.

It was perhaps the English understanding of the term "orangery" that enabled this development to take place without creating conflict. In 1629 John Parkinson, in *Paradisi in sole paradisus terrestris*, recommended that the orange, along with jasmine and the pomegranate, should be grown in containers, and stored in a closed gallery during the winter months. In 1664 John Evelyn published his treatise *Kalendarium Hortense*, in which the various methods for ensuring the survival of tender plants are clearly described. He became the first to use the term "greenhouse" – and also "conservatory" – to describe a building intended exclusively for ornamental plants.[4] He makes a distinction between these and the so-called "stove houses" which were used to force plants in the kitchen gardens. The term "greenhouse" became widely used at this time and corresponded to the French orangery, while up to the second half of the eighteenth century the term "orangery" continued to refer specifically to an orange tree garden.[5]

Once the term became established the purpose of these buildings also required definition. In 1696 Thomas Langford, in *On Fruit Trees*, stated that greenhouses were as much part of the ornamentation of a garden as shelters for tender plants. And that once these curiosities were moved into the garden for the summer the building could also serve as a reception room.[6]

In England the term "greenhouse" gave the orangery a more comprehensive function, enabling it to be used to house all manner of tender plants and not simply the traditional orange, bay, myrtle, and pomegranate trees. It is easy to understand this development given England's maritime expansion during the seventeenth century, accompanied by intensive scientific activity – further fostered by the charter granted to the Royal Society in 1662 for the improvement of the understanding of Nature.[7] Professional specialists such as doctors, naturalists, and apothecaries, and also many non-professional enthusiasts, developed a veritable infatuation with overseas plants from both the East and West Indies. Although relations with the Orient had been established as early as 1600, when the East India Company was granted a trading monopoly with ports in Africa and Asia, for a century the owners of the great estates continued to turn to Dutch horticulturalists for seeds and plants from warmer climates. In 1668 the Triple Alliance between England, the United Dutch Provinces, and Sweden gave this trade a further boost.

Gardeners and nurserymen in the Low Countries were past masters at creating new varieties, particularly with plants grown from bulbs. In addition the botanical gardens of the Low Countries, such as the Doctors' Garden at Leiden created in 1587 by Charles de L'Escluse and the garden in Amsterdam created in 1642 by Dr Jan Commelin, possessed the finest collections of rare species from India and Asia.[8]

Although the flora of the East Indies continued to be relatively inaccessible, that of the Americas soon came within English reach thanks to the regular connections that the Virginia Company established in 1624 with the territories of this name, which were the first "royal colonies".

The directors of the new British botanical gardens – the Oxford Physic Garden, which began to function in 1632, and the Chelsea Physic Garden, created by the Society of Apothecaries in 1673[9] – and wealthy collectors were quick to send researchers to explore Virginia, Carolina, and Georgia in search of new plants. In 1678 the bishop of London, Henry Compton, asked John Baptist Banister, a young missionary, to send him unusual plants from these colonies for the Bishop's Palace at Fulham. He introduced into England *Rhododendrum viscosum*, the purple flowers of *Dodecatheon meadia*, and, most significantly, the first magnolia, *Magnolia virginiana* or *Magnolia glauca* with its lightly fragrant blossom. Other American varieties of the magnolia were not introduced until the next century: notably *Magnolia grandiflora* with its heady fragrance[10] and *Magnolia acuminata*, sent back by the celebrated horticultural botanist John Bartram in 1736. It was to these that specialists creating new varieties owe their greatest success.

The increase in regular supplies of plants from the New World from the 1730s onwards was principally due to the fruitful seed trade developed by Bartram, first with the son of a London draper, Peter Collinson, and later with the master gardeners of the botanical gardens in London and Oxford. On his arrival in Philadelphia in 1728 the botanist had introduced species from all the English colonies on the east coast as well as from the Greater and Lesser Antilles. Bartram enabled more than two thousand new varieties to be introduced into Great Britain and in 1765 was named by George III as the first – and last – botanist royal of North America.[11]

This influx of rare plants now arriving from every continent was of great benefit to botanical gardens but of greater benefit still to horticulturalists and nurserymen, who continued to prosper. The first nursery garden was created in 1681 in Brompton Park, Kensington, and by 1730 around a hundred others had followed in London and the surrounding counties. Even Philip Miller, the master gardener of the Chelsea Physic Garden celebrated for his *Gardeners' Dictionary*, converted part of the garden into a flourishing nursery, where he trained specialists to satisfy the demand from the great English estates.[12] The orangery took on a new significance, becoming central to and a reflection of one of the English aristocracy's greatest passions: the collection of curiosities. Only the orangery could provide a suitable environment for their collections.

At this period, the end of the seventeenth century, collectors were more concerned with the quality of the building rather than its appearance, in view of the prohibitive cost of glass, which was subject to heavy taxation. The buildings were small, with thick masonry walls and narrow, double-glazed windows on the south side; the raised roof was used as a loft and insulated the plants from the cold; one or more cast-iron stoves were also used to maintain a constant temperature. Any ornamentation of the façade remained very simple except in the case of a commission from the royal household or from nobility attached to the court. Following the abdication of James II in 1688, his daughter Mary and her husband, the stadtholder

Croome Court
Worcestershire
Robert Adam
Temple Greenhouse, 1760
decorative motif on the pediment

William of Orange, subsequently William III, brought a number of Dutch plant specialists with them to England. These plantsmen introduced the nobility to a new style of garden, encouraging the fashion for orangeries and their construction on a scale hitherto undreamt of.

The first orangery of this type was commissioned by the King who, in about 1690, asked Christopher Wren to build a long wing at Hampton Court to house the tender plants he had arranged to be brought over from the Low Countries. He was soon followed by the Secretary of State for War, William Blathwayt. As a young man Blathwayt had first held the post of secretary to William Temple, ambassador at The Hague, then to the Duke of Richmond in Denmark, enabling him to get to know not only the countries of northern Europe but also France and Italy. Shortly after his return to England he was appointed auditor of overseas plantations and it was in this position that he became familiar with and developed a passion for the new species recently introduced into Great Britain. In 1692, following his marriage to the heiress to the Dyrham estate, he engaged William Talman, a disciple of Wren, to convert the old manor house and, around 1701, to build a large extension inspired by the orangery at Versailles. Talman, who was also a keen admirer of Jules Hardouin-Mansart, imitated the Italian-style roof and the tall round-headed windows divided by double columns of Tuscan order.[13]

The French design, frequently adopted by the aristocracy, gave the new extension elegance, its classical design harmonizing perfectly with the style of the main building. Only Queen Anne, successor to William and Mary, who was well known for her insularity and uncompromising Englishness,[14] failed to succumb to the French influence. She commissioned Nicholas Hawksmoor (not Vanbrugh, to whom the building is often attributed[15]) to design the new orangery at Kensington Palace, thus ensuring that it would be free from the influence of Versailles. From his first commission in 1702 – an annex to the Royal Naval Hospital at Greenwich built by Christopher Wren – Hawksmoor had shown his determination to avoid conforming to the classical repertoire established by his mentor, Vanbrugh.

The very revolution in garden design that in France created a certain disregard for the orangery produced the opposite effect in England. Since the beginning of the century poets and essayists had been pleading for garden design to become more closely associated with the pictorial arts and to distance itself from the rules of ordonnance copied from architecture. Moreover, they insisted that garden design should incorporate an element essential to landscape painting, the "eye-catcher" or decorative structure. The allusion provided by a temple, rotunda or colonnade increased the atmospheric power of the composition by recalling a lost civilization. In fact it was more for the pleasure of allusion, without which art would be dull, than for the simple pleasures of the senses, that architectural features of this type became popular.[16]

From the mid-eighteenth century these devices began to appear in the designs created for the English nobility by landscape gardeners such as William Kent and Capability Brown. Architects like William Chambers, James Paine, Robert Adam, and Henry Holland felt free to treat the orangery as an essential item and to include it in the wide repertoire of structures available to them. The orangery's original function of protecting rare plants, rather than imposing restrictions on its siting and treatment – as was the case with most functional structures – in fact gave it a unique legitimacy. Its very nature allowed the building to be reinterpreted in a variety of ways, preventing it from becoming simply a place of relaxation where no demands would be made on the imagination.

All interpretations were possible, from the highly classical to the exotic, provided that in each case the building reflected the pleasures, taste, and interests of its owner.

Once it was accepted that the garden should, first and foremost, be a reflection of the "natural order", enthusiasts wanted to discover the laws and mechanisms governing and structuring the natural world and to collect the elements of which it was composed, such as fossils, minerals, animals, and rare plants. Enquiring minds kept abreast of the latest news from the Royal Scientific Society, and the famous Grand Tour, an essential experience of the period, did much to educate their tastes and sensibilities. They frequently returned from the tour, if not with masterpieces, then at least with a number of copies and exquisite *vedute* executed specifically for English clientele. According to Jonathan Richardson, author of *An Argument in behalf of the Science of a Connoisseur*, the art enthusiast or connoiseur (for whom the work was written) had not only the advantage of discovering in paintings and drawings a beauty invisible to the ordinary eye, but also the opportunity of applying this perception to beauty in Nature itself, and to observe in its fine shapes and colours the charming effects of light and shade and the ever-present inspiration to thought...[17]

One result of the fashion for viewing nature through art was that some collectors sought to create an environment which could bring immediate satisfaction to the senses – with the fragrance of a flower or the taste of exotic fruit – and also yield the more subtle pleasures of the mind inspired by the contemplation of a rare object imbued with history. Their aim was to bring together in one place the three "universes" they felt compelled to possess: *Naturalia* – with its bewitching taste of unfamiliar, distant lands; *Artificialia* – the canvases and etchings of the masters evoking the memory of Roman landscapes much travelled in search of antiquities; and the world of *Antiquitas* itself.[18]

The most imposing orangeries constructed during the second half of the eighteenth century were built to satisfy these different needs. The orangeries at Bowood House, Margam, Warwick Castle, and Woburn Abbey are excellent examples of this desire to create a "showcase of curiosities".

To provide a style worthy of such an undertaking architects turned to the buildings of antiquity for inspiration and to architects such as Andrea Palladio, who had reinterpreted the classical repertoire with such success.

Robert Adam, in particular, discovered that this repertoire provided him with all the elements he needed to refine the concept of the orangery to such a point that it became a mere "suggestion" of the original. At the age of twenty-six the young architect, like all cultivated Englishmen, had undertaken an educational journey which had led him to Italy and to the newly studied archaeological sites there. He was fascinated by the ruins of Pompeii, the excavation of which began in 1748, but even more so by the remains of the Palace of Diocletian at Salona just outside Split.[19]

In 1760 Adam received his first commission to build an orangery – at Croome Court for the Earl of Coventry – and immediately adopted a style that used features characteristic of a temple: the hexastyle portico with Doric columns that supported a vast pediment crowning almost the entire façade. These distinctive features enabled him to raise the orangery to the rank of Temple Greenhouse. Adam adopted the same style for other commissions: at Kenwood for the Earl of Mansfield in 1764 and at Bowood House in 1769 for the future Marquess of Landsdowne. The orangery had now become an essential feature on every estate and, although it may have complied with Adam's rules of appearance, its role was not always so purely representational. It developed from providing a focal point in the landscape that would draw the eye towards the distant view over the countryside beyond – the role assigned it by Capability Brown at Broadlands – into a pleasure pavilion and even a small "folly".

Adam, in common with various architects during the second half of the eighteenth century, also succumbed to this temptation. In 1780 at Osterley Manor he extended the long gallery in which plants were housed by creating a garden room, a small semicircular room which is in fact all that remains today. At Mamhead House he demonstrated his consummate skill in combining the two requirements by designing a Palladian rotunda which could be used equally well as a dining room or for housing orange trees. At

Frampton Court the neo-Gothic orangery is a garden folly, whereas at Weston Park James Paine, Adam's great rival, transforms it into an elegant *palazzina* with concealed rooms.

Robert Adam, James Paine, Henry Holland, and William Chambers were architects who took Addison's remark about the pleasure of allusion to heart; the buildings they designed provided a clear archetype that was adopted and copied many times regardless of the purpose for which the building was intended, which may have been to house a collection or simply to provide a decorative structure or folly in the landscape. As a result the orangery became fixed by architects in a formalism that was increasingly incompatible with a more modern concept of design.

Before the end of the century plant specialists began to demand more air and light in buildings designed to house plants and were highly critical of heavy pediments and overstated columns. In 1718 Richard Bradley, a professor of botany at Cambridge, had advocated the use of a glass dome roof, although at this point no mention was made of the light refraction principle. He provided a very clear illustration of the design in the new edition of his treatise entitled *New Improvements of Planting and Gardening*, published in 1731.[20] Although this idea was not put into practice until the end of the century certain landowners were already showing interest in the importance of the penetration of light to plant cultivation. Lady Boringdon at Saltram was

Margram
West Glamorgan, Wales
Anthony Keck
Orangery, 1787
cornice detail

one of these and, to improve the environment for the orange trees she had imported from Genoa at great expense in 1773, she ordered the round-headed windows to be replaced by rectangular sash windows that completely filled the intercolumniation along the whole façade.

However, it was not until the following century that architects, cognisant of the possibilities offered by the new materials then available, such as iron and cast iron, designed buildings in which form and function were in total harmony.

A similar rationalism also led the English to re-examine the somewhat frivolous role played by the eighteenth-century greenhouse (to some extent the product of French influence) in plant cultivation. This building was now commonly known as an orangery, and in some cases even by the French term *orangerie*.

A Necessity and a Delight

In England the orangery became an indispensable part of every royal home and, from the earliest eighteenth-century examples, all combined elegance with pleasure and a practical purpose.

The building's double purpose harmonized well with both the political and personal views of Queen Anne. In 1704 she commissioned John Vanbrugh's assistant, Nicholas Hawksmoor, to construct an orangery near Kensington Palace which would be clearly differentiated from the palace by its architecture, position, and function. The new building satisfied the queen's liking for the Dutch style and also her keen nationalism. The orangery was built facing the royal residence rather than as an extension of the main building.

Queen Anne found the orangery an enchanting place in which to "entertain her favourites". The queen's principal favourite at the period was Sarah Churchill, and she bestowed lavish presents on her including, in 1704, the estate of Woodstock and sufficient funds for the court architects, John Vanbrugh and Nicholas Hawksmoor, to build the magnificent Blenheim Palace on the estate.

As far as the orangery was concerned Vanbrugh took a traditional approach and extended the main palace building, as Wren had done at Hampton Court and Talman at Dyrham, with a long, slightly recessed gallery; this was completed in 1707 and at the Duchess's request a delightful flower garden was created alongside. However, Lady Sarah had a disagreement with the Queen in 1710 and went into exile two years later when the Duke was accused of embezzlement. On her return, differences between her and Vanbrugh prevented her from enjoying its delights.

The orangery at Blenheim became a theatre in 1750 until the end of the nineteenth century when the French landscape gardener Achille Duchêne covered it with a glass roof and added an Italian-style garden.

Kensington Palace
London
Nicholas Hawksmoor
Orangery, 1704–1705

ABOVE:
interior
LEFT:
main entrance

FACING PAGE:
Blenheim Palace
Oxfordshire
John Vanbrugh
Orangery, 1704–1707
general view and Italian garden
designed by Achille Duchêne

Chatsworth
Derbyshire
William Talman
Orangery, 1698

Above:
view from the loggia
Facing page:
general view

Right:
Dyrham Park
Avon
William Talman
Orangery, c. 1701
lithograph, c. 1845

A Showcase for Curiosities

During the second half of the eighteenth century attitudes changed and some orangery owners looked on these fine buildings not as spaces for entertainment or the pursuit of horticulture but as places where the "natural" and the "artificial" could live happily alongside one another and satisfy their passion for collecting.

In 1768 Robert Adam was commissioned by Lord William, Earl of Shelburne to design an orangery for his house at Bowood that would not simply be a "showcase for curiosities" but would itself rank as a "collector's item". Adam turned for inspiration to a work that had always fascinated him, the Palace of Diocletian at Salona, near the port of Split on the Adriatic. The exceptional quality of the new wing enabled it to survive the financial problems faced by the estate, unlike the house, which was demolished in 1955.

On its completion in 1769 the Earl, as planned, turned the impressive orangery built by Adam into a "showcase for curiosities" in which he could indulge his passion for collecting. One of the wings became a magnificent library with decor designed by the architect himself, and the chemist Joseph Priestley was appointed as librarian. The Earl took a great interest in Priestley's work and had a laboratory installed for him behind the long plant gallery; it was here that Priestley made some of his major discoveries. In 1773 he isolated a large number of gases, including oxygen, and was the first scientist to elucidate the respiratory system of plants.

The Earl, made Marquess of Landsdowne in 1784, was a talented politician who took a keen interest in the economic and scientific development of the country but he was also a connoisseur of art, and once the orangery was complete he converted the other wing, which he had originally intended to use as a menagerie, into an art museum housing the collection of marble statuary he had brought back from his frequent trips to Italy.

Bowood House
Wiltshire
Robert Adam
Orangery, 1769
lower terrace, redesigned by John Kennedy, 1851

ABOVE:
aedicule feature
LEFT:
interior
FACING PAGE:
general view

In 1772 Thomas Mansel Talbot, who owned the vast Margam estate in Wales, returned from a Grand Tour with some of the finest items in his collection. However, when, in 1787, he commissioned Anthony Keck, a local architect, to build an orangery completely separate from the main house he did not intend this solely as a place to exhibit his precious collection. The orangery built by Keck was the largest in Britain and one huge gallery was set aside for orange trees, which the Earl himself looked after with great care. According to family records orange trees had been cultivated at Margam since the end of the sixteenth century when Philip II of Spain's ships had broken up against the cliffs on the Glamorgan coast shedding, among other things, their precious cargo of fruit trees that the Spanish king had been sending to Elizabeth I.

Keck indicates the twin functions of the orangery by treating the façades in very different ways. The central section, used to house tender plants, is bonded with vermiculated bossage echoing the fact that items within are from nature, whereas the two side pavilions, one used as a library and the other for *objets d'art,* are distinguished by the Palladian style of their architecture with pediments and Venetian windows.

Lord George Greville, whose home was Warwick Castle, commissioned the architect William Eboral to build an orangery overlooking the new gardens at the castle. His nephew Sir William Hamilton, ambassador at the court of Naples, had presented him with a Roman vase dating from the second century AD which had been found during excavations at the Villa Hadriana. Eboral's Noble Greenhouse, constructed in 1788, was to provide a home for this piece where it could be shown to its best advantage. The building was of a plain design, with tall, pointed-arch windows fitted with the purest, most expensive glass from the glassworks in Bristol. On his visit to the gardens of Warwick Castle in 1829 the famous landscape gardener, Claudius Loudon, bemoans the fact that plants were now no more than a cosmetic detail and describes the orangery as having an opaque roof (which was glazed during the following century) and being disfigured by feeble specimens of pelargoniums and other very common plants.

Warwick Castle
Warwickshire
William Eboral
Orangery, 1788

ABOVE:
south façade detail
FACING PAGE:
general view

LEFT:
John Brandard
Warwick Castle vase
lithograph, 1840

Margram
West Glamorgan, Wales
Anthony Keck
Orangery, 1787–1793

Above:
interior
Left:
Venetian window on the porch

Margram
West Glamorgan, Wales
Anthony Keck
Orangery, 1787–1793

Right:
south façade detail
Below:
transverse view

The Orangery as Temple

There is nothing to distinguish the decorative temple by William Chambers for the gardens at Kew from the orangery by Capability Brown on the estate at Broadlands. The similarity was deliberate and was Brown's response to his critics. Chambers himself had criticized Brown for creating landscapes that were devoid of art, servile copies of nature little better than open grassland.

As a young man in 1741 Brown had worked as assistant gardener at Stowe and had been introduced by William Kent, the grand master of the picturesque landscape, to the art of directing the eye of the viewer towards specific areas of the landscape through the use of "eye-catchers" or decorative structures. Kent had been a painter and interior designer before becoming a garden architect, and for his first commission – at Chiswick in 1719 – he transformed the orange garden into a stunning theatre in the classical style with wide terraces converging onto a small rotunda. All his work, at Claremont, Rousham, and Stowe demonstrated his architect's talent for, as Horace Walpole described it, creating vistas of exquisite taste.

When, in 1767, Brown was commissioned by Viscount Palmerston to redesign the gardens at Broadlands, he remembered the lessons his master had taught him. Exceptionally, his design was to include a decorative structure that would, however, not be devoid of purpose, nor disturb the overall composition of the grounds. The orangery provided Brown with the ideal justification for his decision. Yet by leaving only the temple portico exposed – the main body of the building being concealed behind a clump of trees – the decorative touch is so light as to be almost transparent, not troubling the eye but leading it towards some distant vision of Elysian fields.

Facing page:
Broadlands
Hampshire
Capability Brown
Orangery, 1767
side portico

Above:
Kew Gardens
London
William Chambers
gardens, created 1757–1763
temple

Right:
Chiswick House
London
Pieter Rysbrack
Orange garden at Chiswick House, c. 1730

Croome Court
Worcestershire
Robert Adam
Temple Greenhouse, 1760

A Dual Role for the Orangery

The orangery now served two functions: it gave an added charm to the "follies" in the grounds of stately homes and provided an excuse and venue for amorous meetings. The orangery now became a peaceful retreat – as at Frampton Court. Built after 1740 for Richard Clutterbuck the style of the orangery is so similar to the designs that appear in *Chinese and Gothic Architecture Properly Ornamented,* a catalogue of garden structures by William Halfpenny, that it could well have been his work.

Another architect who demonstrated considerable skill in combining orangery and folly was James Paine. Drawing on the bucolic influences of mythology he gave the orangery a style better suited to its romantic role. The orange tree hall in the Temple of Diana – as Paine called the orangery at Weston Park – has an unmistakable Italian atmosphere with its slender Ionic columns and Pompeii-inspired ceiling decorated with foliage, garlands, and scrolls. As a final touch, behind the hall the architect has concealed two small rooms, a mu-sic room and a room for taking tea, decorated with panels depicting the goddess Diana and her lovers.

The fashion in France at this time for Anglo-Chinese gardens created a vogue for garden follies, but the orangery never became part of this development. Although at Ménars the architect Jacques-Germain Soufflot, who was landscaping the park for the Marquis de Marigny, brother of the great Marquise de Pompadour, found an elegant device for including, among the more fanciful structures of the gardens, an orangery still intended to fulfil its original function. At one end he built a magnificent rotunda, the Temple d'Abondance, terminating the upper terrace of the château. Through a clever use of corridors and stairs this room connects the château with the orangery. The orangery itself is in a sober style as befits its original function and is therefore discreetly situated on a lower level. Soufflot succeeded, through the use of rationality, in creating a subtle combination of the serious and the frivolous.

Park at the Château de Ménars
Val de Loire
Jacques-Germain Soufflot
Orangery and Abundance Rotunda, c. 1770

ABOVE:
orangery façade, detail
LEFT:
Adam the Elder
Abundance

Park at the Château de Ménars
Val de Loire
Jacques-Germain Soufflot
Orangery and Abundance Rotunda, c. 1770

LEFT:
monumental vase
BELOW:
view of rotunda and orangery

Frampton Court
Gloucestershire
Gothic orangery, post 1740

FACING PAGE:
south façade
RIGHT:
general view of the pool

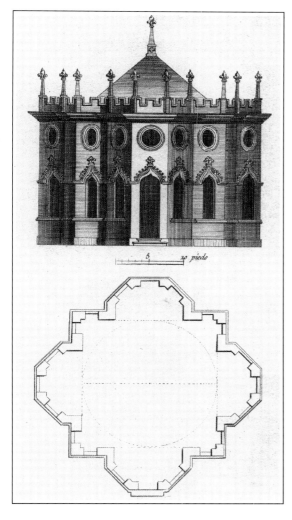

ABOVE AND RIGHT:
Georges-Louis Le Rouge
Jardins anglo-chinois à la mode, 1774–1789
Kiosks by Halfpenny

Mamhead Park
Devon
attributed to Robert Adam
Orangery, c. 1765

Left:
cupola lantern
Facing page:
general view

Above and left:
Georges-Louis Le Rouge
Jardins anglo-chinois à la mode, 1774–1789
rotunda pavilions

Weston Park
Staffordshire
James Paine
Orangery, Temple of Diana, c. 1760

<small>ABOVE:</small>
general view
<small>LEFT:</small>
Diana and Endymion
decorative panels in the tea room

Weston Park
Staffordshire
James Paine
Orangery, Temple of Diana, c. 1760

RIGHT:
Diana and her Nymphs
decorative panels in the tea room
BELOW:
interior

Weston Park
Staffordshire
James Paine
Orangery, Temple of Diana, c. 1760
Ionic capitals

ABOVE:
internal
FACING PAGE:
external

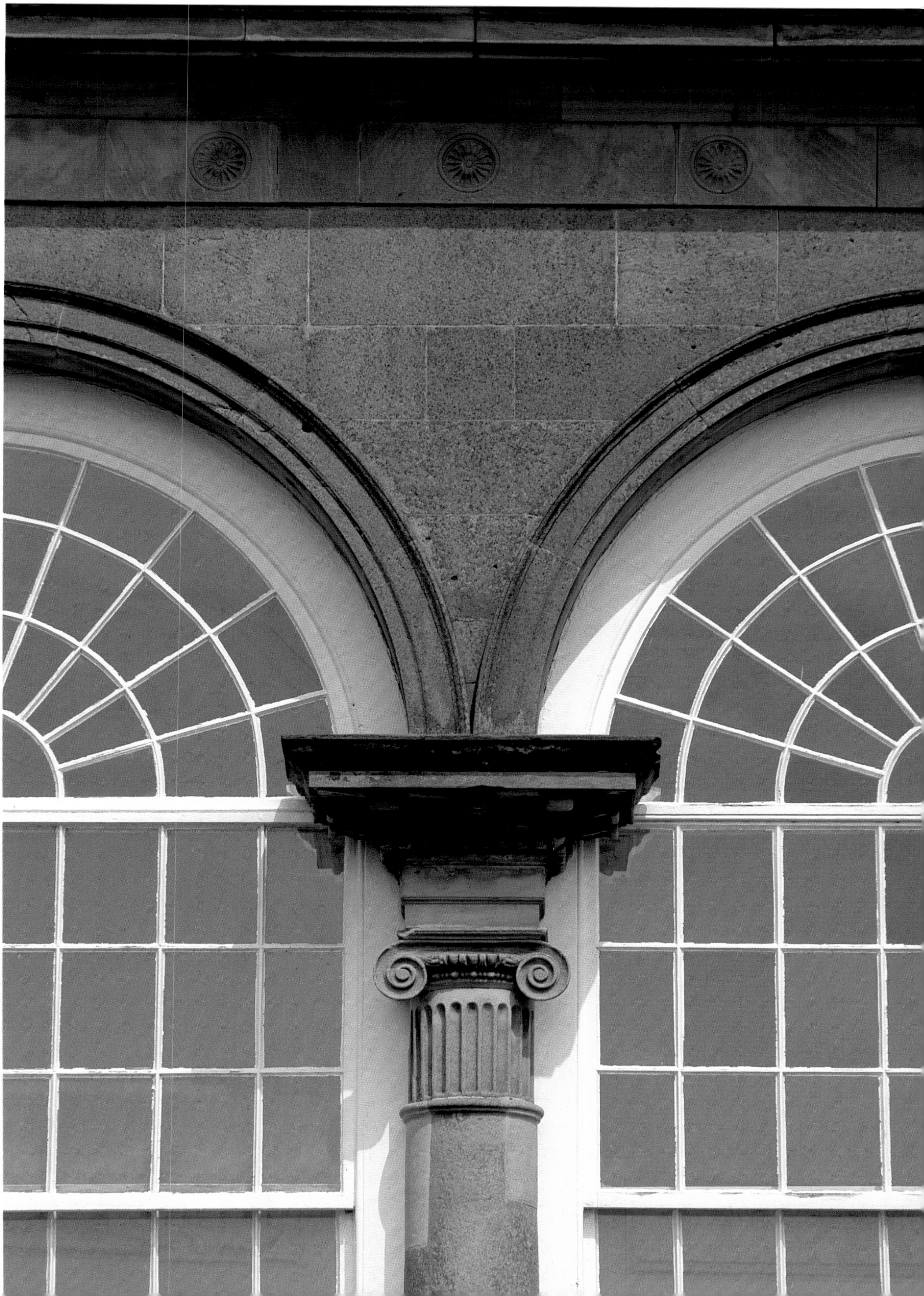

The Move to a New Austerity

In 1757 the Dowager Princess Augusta and her son The Prince of Wales, later to become George III, commissioned the young architect William Chambers to redesign the gardens at Kew and to incorporate the "eye-catchers" fashionable at the time, such as temples, pagodas, mosques, Chinese-style aviaries, etc.

Somewhat unexpectedly, and contrary to the general trend of the period, Chambers also included an orangery designed with simple lines and without ornamentation. In fact the idea had come from John Stuart, Earl of Bute, close friend of the princess and eminent botanist. The rationale of the design was the requirements of the plants the building would house, so the façades were left free of colonnades, porticos, or porches but retained the classical round-headed windows. This produced a light and spacious interior suitable for the country's most exotic species. When his mother died in 1772 George III appointed Sir Joseph Banks, who had returned the year before from a voyage around the world on James Cook's ship *Endeavour*, superintendent of the estate. All the plants brought back from Cook's circumnavigations of the globe were now given to Kew, which in 1760 had been established as the Royal Botanic Gardens. By the end of the century Kew Gardens held 5,500 species, inventoried in 1789 by the master-gardener William Aiton in his substantial work *Hortus Kewensis*. And in the same year the first variety of magnolia from Asia bloomed; this was *Magnolia denudata*, native to the mountains of Yunnan province in China.

England had already admired the beauty of the American varieties of the magnolia, including *Magnolia virginiana* and *Magnolia grandiflora* in plates produced by botanical illustrators, including Georg Dionysius Ehret, one of the most celebrated botanical illustrators of the period.

Christoph Jakob Trew
Plantae selectae, 1750–1773
illustrations by Georg Dionysius Ehret

ABOVE:
Magnolia virginiana
FACING PAGE:
Magnolia maxima flora

LEFT:
Kew Gardens, Princess Augusta of Wales gardens
London
William Chambers
Orangery, 1761
general view

At the Chelsea Physic Garden (to which he was introduced by Philip Miller) and the Royal Botanic Gardens at Kew, Ehret executed magnificent plates which he sent to his German patron, Christoph Trew, a wealthy doctor. The marvellous six-volume work entitled *Plantae selectae*, published by Trew between 1750 and 1773, was composed of these plates.

Some garden enthusiasts, following the example set by Lord Bute, began to adopt a new style of orangery more in keeping with its function. But although they were keen to implement specialist recommendations on the need for more air and light they also remained loyal to the Palladian style Adam used so effectively.

Thus in 1768 when Lord Boringdon decided to refurbish Saltram House, the family residence near Plymouth, it was Adam he commissioned. His wife, Lady Theresa Parker, also consulted Adam regarding the construction of a wooden orangery to the west of the main house in 1775. Lady Parker, a woman of taste, wanted the building to have a classical elegance that would be in harmony with the family residence. Nevertheless she accepted the advice of her head gardener and agreed that the portico and side wings should be on a level plane to avoid shading the plants. The façade with its huge double-hung sash windows is very open, allowing sunlight to penetrate deep into the room.

During the same period, on another Devon estate – Bicton Hall, one of the greatest estates in the region – the owner, Dennys Rolle, also managed to combine attraction with necessity. He chose as the setting for his new orangery the French-style garden designed by his brother Henry Rolle around 1730. From the central loggia, similar in style to Adam's Temple Greenhouse, the formal gardens slope gently down towards a green bordered by a large ornamental pond. Rolle, who was passionate about botany, also had two side wings built extending the loggia, but lower in height. These imposing structures housed the traditional container-grown shrubs but also many varieties of palm and banana trees; Rolle had been one of the first to bring these over from Florida, where he owned a large estate.

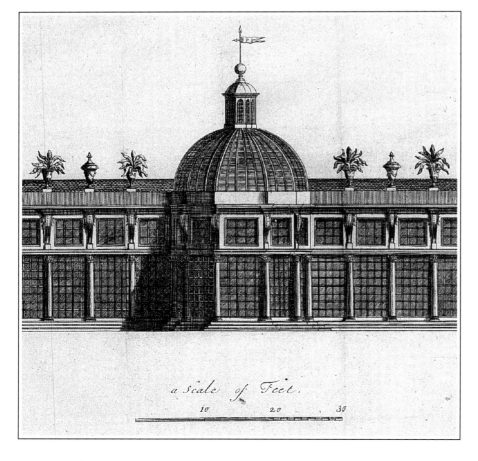

a scale of Feet.

Bicton Hall
Devon
Gardens, created c. 1730

Above:
general view of the gardens
Orangery, c. 1770
Facing page:
south façade

Left:
Richard Bradley
New Improvements of Planting, 1731
Greenhouse elevation

Saltram House
Devon
Orangery, 1775

FACING PAGE:
interior
ABOVE:
central portico detail
RIGHT:
general view

ANANAS aculeatus,
fructu ovato, carne albida
Plumerii, Tournef. Inst. p. 650.

Final Interpretations – from the Classic to the Outrageous

When André Thevet published his work *Les singularités de la France antarctique autrement nommé Amérique* in 1558 one of the marvels from Brazil that he revealed to his French readership was the pineapple. Thevet was a chaplain from Angoulême and had discovered the fruit's excellent qualities between 1555 and 1556, while spending some months at Fort Coligny, a French colony on a small island off Rio de Janeiro.

Until the eighteenth century naturalists were undecided what to call the fruit; all, however, were united in acknowledging the unique taste and flavour of its flesh. Despite its fine qualities the pineapple was not cultivated in England or France until the beginning of the eighteenth century when Dutch hot houses came into more widespread use. Only structures such as these with their tall sloping frames, built against a wall and heated by stoves, could provide the temperature between 20° and 30° C (68° and 86° F) needed for the slow fruiting of the offsets planted in layers and covered with tanbark.

It was claimed that in England Charles II's head gardener, John Rose, had already succeeded, in 1676, in obtaining fruit from shoots collected on Barbados. However, it seems more likely that this honour fell to the director of the East India Company, Sir Matthew Decker, in 1720. In France it was 1735 before Louis XV was given the first French-grown pineapples.

The sudden passion for the cultivation of the pineapple was as brief as it was intense. It achieved its most spectacular expression in the folly built in 1761 for the fourth Earl of Dunmore, on his estate near Stirling. The architect, about whom nothing is known, paid the most eloquent homage to the fruit by reproducing it with astonishing realism and on an enormous scale as the roof to a charming pavilion.

Christoph Jakob Trew
Plantae selectae, 1750–1773
illustrations by Georg Dionysius Ehret

FACING PAGE:
Ananas aculeatus...
ABOVE:
Ananas folio vix serrato...

RIGHT:
Veitshöchheim
Bavaria
gardens of the Prince-Bishops of Würzburg
Ferdinand Tietz
Oriental kiosk, 1768

Dunmore Park
Stirlingshire (Scotland)
Pineapple House, 1761

ABOVE:
north façade
FACING PAGE:
south façade

LEFT:
Hot houses on the south façade
lithograph, c. 1920

4

CULTIVATION AND COLLECTION

Plant collections on display in palaces of glass

> How I delight to see these sanctuaries, these transparent shelters,
> conceal from the climate their diverse offerings –
> the asylum quicken the Iberian jasmine,
> and allow the frail periwinkle to forget its homeland;
> and the yellow pineapple, deceived by heat,
> yield up its fruit, treasured usurped...

By 1782, when the Abbé Delille was describing the delights of the "transparent shelter" in his poem *Les Jardins ou l'Art d'embellir le paysage* [1] the orangery was already in decline. The new craze in Europe was for the hot house. A detailed study of the development of the hot house is not possible within the confines of this work; however, a brief investigation of its original purpose and the methods of construction and design adopted will help us to understand the development of the conservatory – one of the most interesting variations on the orangery the nineteenth century was to produce.

By the middle of the seventeenth century glass structures for the protection of young plants and where flowers and fruit could be brought on early were no longer a novelty. Horticulturists recommended that tender plants should be placed in special frames. These were enclosed structures, with tall, sloping lights mounted in oak frames, installed against the south-facing wall of the kitchen garden to ensure the plants received maximum light. In 1640 these structures were given the name "serre" in France.

The steaming manure in these frames encouraged growth but before long fires fed from outside were being used to provide extra heat. Some gardeners were already seeking a way to remedy the uneven distribution of heat due to the spacing out of heat sources. In England the essayist John Evelyn, in the 1691 edition of his treatise *Kalendarium Hortense*, had proposed a system based on the temperature regulation of circulating air; however, it was never developed. [2] At the beginning of the seventeenth century the Dutch perfected an indirect heating system; this technique remained in common use until the following century and was also installed in certain orangeries. The system's efficiency was further improved by the installation of baffles, which doubled air flow time, turning the whole wall into a heater. [3]

In France the term "serre chaude" did not come into common use until 1762. In the 1765 edition of Diderot and d'Alembert's *Encyclopédie* it is still defined as "a type of room, preferably facing south, with many openings to allow sunlight to enter, and enclosed by double-glazed doors and windows"; the definition is rather imprecise and does little to differentiate the hot house from the orangery. The authors also advise that "Dutch and English greenhouses should be used as models, as our nation has still only limited knowledge of types of building such as these, dedicated to the advancement of botany". [4]

These shelters soon became a real necessity: at the end of the previous century explorations had begun to bring back flora from overseas and these activities had increased with the development of the Jardin du Roi and the work of its superintendent, Guy Crescent Fagon, who was the first to encourage Louis XIV and his ministers to take an interest in botany.[5] Joseph Pitton de Tournefort's expedition to the Levant between 1700 and 1702 marked the beginning of the first era of great scientific expeditions.

In 1766 Joseph Philibert Commerson took part in the first French circumnavigation of the globe on board *La Boudeuse*, with the botanist Louis Antoine de Bougainville. Among the nearly three thousand new species discovered was *Bougainvillea* from Brazil, the extraordinary flowers of Tahiti or "New Cythera", as it was called, discovered in 1767, unknown varieties of hibiscus, and sweetly fragrant *Gardenia tahitensis*.[6]

In 1769, in his Grapefruit Garden, Pierre Poivre became the first to succeed in growing the clove and the nutmeg – two spices that had been jealously guarded by the Dutch on the Molucca Islands.[7] In 1785 Louis Guillaume Lemmonier encouraged André Michaux to establish a botanical garden and nursery in New York; this was transferred a year later to Charleston in South Carolina. Michaux was now able to supply France with most of the rare American species of which England was the primary source.[8]

By the end of the century amateur botanists were building increasing numbers of hot houses on their estates to cultivate tea, coffee and pineapple plants. "Through the introduction of artificial heat via hidden ducts the hot house can enjoy the pleasures of Spring and a mild temperature. The most tender plants can be grown, the most delightful exotics and early native species. A thin stream of water flowing through and never freezing gives life to this charming scene, which, though artificial, is most pleasant".[9] Even the Prince de Ligne, who, as we have seen, no longer countenanced the formality of container-grown orange trees, considered such places, which would soon find their place at Belœil, a genuine source of delight: "The hot house buildings will be five small pavilions and in their centres there will be ponds of white marble to give variety, water to refresh the eye and the earliest fruits. These will serve as galleries, in which one may stroll in the midst of the wintry weather, leading to a splendid winter garden at the far end."[10]

The French Revolution did not end the aristocratic passion for rare plants, which flourished again under the Consulate. At La Malmaison the future Empress was inspired to create a garden to surpass the Jardin du Roi, which had now been renamed the Muséum d'histoire naturelle. After her marriage to Bonaparte, Josephine was finally able to realize a dream she had held dear: on her new estate, purchased in 1799, she re-created the landscape of Martinique, the "enchanted island" on which she had spent her youth. She wrote to her mother, "Here I have the Alpine soldanella, the Parma violet, the Nile lily, the Damietta rose – conquests from Italy and Egypt that will never make enemies of Bonaparte. And here too is my own triumph – jasmine from Martinique that I planted myself. It reminds me of my home, my childhood, and the adornments of my girlhood...".[11]

In 1803, on the advice of the botanist and director of gardens and greenhouses, Brisseau de Mirbel, Josephine commissioned Jean-Thomas Thibault and Barthélemy Vignon to build new hot houses of a size unprecedented in the gardens of a mere plant enthusiast. These buildings, completed in 1805, were 50 m (165 ft) long and heated by twelve stoves; two years later they were enlarged further by Louis-Martin Berthault, the estate's new landscape gardener. In the words of Chateaubriand he created "a cool and pleasant room, exquisitely furnished, from which one could admire the abundant tropical flora without the discomfort of a stifling atmosphere".[12]

The hot house was built in a very traditional style, its design too close to that of the orangery – which had now become known as a "cold house". It was normally constructed with only one glazed side and did not provide plants with sufficient sunlight, despite its tall windows. The glazing bars also created shadows. The wood used was normally oak, which let in water and draughts, and the single breast wall left the structure vulnerable to high winds. At La Malmaison, "four years after the construction the entire structure had to be shored up to prevent the walls from collapsing".[13]

Such problems were not restricted to hot houses built in France; the same problem had been encountered in England during the previous century. As a result some English greenhouses, including those at Bicton and Saltram, were built with tall hanging sashes that ran from ground level to the cornice.

New developments in English garden design at the beginning of the nineteenth century made it all the more imperative for collectors of rare plants to find a solution to the problem of growing tender plants. Although the work of Capability Brown was still widely admired, some landscape gardeners were now moving in the opposite direction.

In 1795 Humphry Repton, the new authority on garden design, published *Sketches and Hints on Landscape Gardening*, in which he encouraged everyone to take up the new pleasure of gardening.[14] Under his influence the flower garden, fruit garden, and kitchen garden ceased to be mere accessories or the sole domain of horticultural enthusiasts. Before long the orangeries built to house container-grown shrubs, and the hot houses where young plants were sheltered and brought on, were unable to meet the growing demand created by this new fashion. New solutions were needed and an appropriate terminology had to be established. This need was met in Philip Miller's famous dictionary; the final edition of *Miller's Dictionary* (revised and with additions) clarified meanings and the use to which each type of "house" was put.[15] The term "greenhouse", as we have seen, was no longer used to refer to an orangery but to a form of glasshouse. The greenhouse became part of the fruit and vegetable gardens and was used to grow plants in pots for planting out in borders and formal beds. If used to force plants for early flowering or fruiting it became known as a "forcing house". This spawned a variety of terms to describe greenhouses used for specific plants.

The "conservatory", a term transferred directly into French as *conservatoire* by the specialist Pierre Boitard, became an original replacement for the orangery of the previous century, or former greenhouse. Nowadays,

Hot houses by Claude Baudard de Saint-James for the Saint James Folly, c. 1785
wash drawing

unfortunately, the French term is only used to describe the building in which herbaria and other works are kept in a botanical garden.[16]

In England great care was given to the architecture of conservatories. Built either as extensions to existing dwellings or as separate buildings, they always remained part of the pleasure garden. Inside the conservatory plants were grown directly in the soil and arranged to create an indoor garden, hence the term "jardin d'hiver" later used by the French.[17] The conservatory differed from the orangery in the way in which plants were cultivated and also in the variety of its locations; throughout the first half of the nineteenth century the orangery found itself devoid of purpose. During the Victorian period, however, some landowners were unable to resist the temptation to build an orangery in the classical style to adorn the grounds of their estate, in addition to the conservatory already adjoining their stately home. By a rather odd turnaround of events the nineteenth-century English orangery, which was in essence a garden pavilion, became popular again in France in the same period. In 1844 a new orangery was built in the Bagatelle gardens, owned at the time by Lord Seymour, Marquess of Hertford, who was a great friend of Napoleon III. And in 1852 the Emperor himself had an orangery built in the Tuileries gardens, providing a focal point in the long vista of the grounds. Four years later a matching pavilion was built where real tennis was played.[18]

Once the requirements of the buildings were clearly established, architects set about finding designs and structures to meet the demands of increasingly well-informed landowners, many of whom were members of the growing number of horticultural societies, such as the Horticultural Society of London, created in 1804.[19] These enthusiasts wanted not only to ensure that their tender plants were protected during the winter months but also to provide them with a quality of light that would enable even the most delicate species to bloom in all seasons. This requirement, though not new, was certainly on a different scale, and obliged both architects and landscape gardeners to take stock of traditional methods and embrace the possibilities offered by the new techniques and materials produced by Britain's extraordinary economic and industrial development.

Iron production had continued to increase in order to satisfy the demands of this revolution and had found new outlets, especially in the building industry, where previously it had been of little importance. At this stage it was only used in the frames of domes, to strengthen load-bearing lintels, and for hardware. Increased demand resulted in the production of components that were no longer forged individually but cast and rolled in series; these were products that would revolutionize building methods and costs. For three generations the Darby family of Coalbrookdale, a small town in Shropshire, developed this new technology. Firstly, in 1709 Abraham Darby I, the grandfather of the family, had the ingenious idea of using coke in the blast furnaces that dealt with the iron ore, thus eliminating the use of charcoal, which was difficult to obtain and expensive, and of coal, which made the cast iron brittle.[20] In the 1740s his son Abraham Darby II improved the power of the blast furnaces and obtained a more fluid mass that was easier to mould and entirely pressure-resistant. But it was Abraham Darby III, the grandson, who demonstrated the possible applications of cast iron in the building industry. In 1779 the Darby company submitted a much lower bid for the construction of a bridge than the masonry firm with which it was competing and won the order to produce the arches for the first metal bridge ever to be constructed; this was the famous Ironbridge at Coalbrookdale on the Severn, designed by Thomas Farnall Pritchard and opened to traffic two years later.[21]

Cast iron had the advantage of being both waterproof and frost-resistant and architects began to show an interest in using it for buildings to house and protect tender plants. It became clear that a metal structure built from narrow, light components such as pillars, trusses, and ribs, would be able to provide the level of light and ventilation essential in such a building. They also saw it as an opportunity to revitalize their formal repertoire and create a more modern aesthetic, "the aesthetic of iron", based on the transparency of glass.[22] However, they were still confronted by two major but contrasting problems: as a material cast iron was almost too "flexible", and therefore unable to develop a style of its own, while their entire conceptual approach was based on an established system of reference. As a result many new conservatories were caught between the two, and in terms of design the buildings remained very similar to orangeries built during the previous century.

The first innovation involving the use of iron – originally cast iron – came in roof design. Light entered buildings unevenly, the best areas being those next to the glass façades; therefore it followed that the only way to ensure a more even distribution was to provide a translucent roof. The cast-iron trusses developed for use in mills provided an ideal framework. The frame was light and almost completely transparent; rings placed between the main

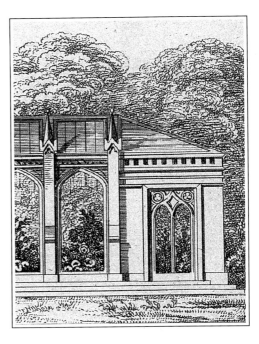

Pierre Boitard
Traité de la composition et de l'ornement des jardins, 1839
English orangery (detail)

tie and the principal provided an elegant form of reinforcement and the roof lights could be fitted directly in it. In some cases internal pillars, also made of cast iron, were used to increase the span of the trusses and relieve the load from the masonry-built façade bearers. They were often hollow and could be used for rainwater drainage. As they were cast in separate sections they were easy to install and offered architects a wide range of ornamental possibilities. Light entered through the translucent roof and through the tall sash windows, which were still made with wooden frames to prevent too much heat loss. Only the north façade was still a solid wall, as in the orangery, reflecting heat and light and concealing workrooms and heating equipment.

"Model conservatories" of this type were designed by John Nash for Barnsley Park in 1806, and by Jeffrey Wyatville for Belton House in 1815, while the publication in 1816 of Humphry Repton's treatise entitled *Fragments on the Theory and Practice of Landscape Gardening* made them more widely known. These buildings were so obviously the successors to the orangery that in France they became known as "English orangeries" and were still being built in a number of gardens on the Continent at the end of the nineteenth century.[23] However, some horticultural experts, such as Sir George Mackenzie and the famous landscape gardener and architect John Claudius Loudon, were already expressing doubts about conservatories with vertical sides, even if they had a glass roof. In 1815 Mackenzie, who was a member of the Horti-cultural Society, wrote an article on the style of glazing required to provide forcing houses with sufficient light, in which he demonstrated the advant-ages of designing structures in semi- or quarter-circles.[24] Three years later Loudon built the first curvilinear structures at his Bayswater property near London. This was a turning point in the popularity of the greenhouse but marked a departure away from buildings deriving from the conservatory.[25]

Curiously though, Loudon did not lose interest in what he considered to be the more traditional type of greenhouse and even invented a system to improve it. He demonstrated the new system in 1822 but, although it had indisputable advantages such as standardized components and a rigid struc-ture, not shared by pitched roofs or even curvilinear glasshouses, Loudon was not the first to make use of it.

The first to experiment with the new ridge and furrow roof was the sixth Duke of Devonshire's young master gardener, Joseph Paxton. He took credit for the new system after patenting it in 1850. However, although the system was modern, Paxton remained traditional in his use of materials, favouring wood over iron. In fact he continued to use wood for all his build-ings as he was concerned about the high thermal conductivity of iron and the additional heating costs that would result.[26] Paxton left the family farm as a young man and was first employed by the Horticultural Society, main-taining the gardens at Chiswick House. In 1826 the Duke of Devonshire, himself a member of the Society, took note of the young gardener's ability and put him in charge of reorganizing the planting on his Chatsworth estate. In 1832 Paxton at last put his celebrated system into practice to mod-ernize the Chatsworth orangery, which had been built in 1698 by William Talman. Between the closely-spaced purlins he placed light, saw-tooth pat-tern lights exactly equal in size. The girders were shaped to act as gutters, collecting the rainwater that drained into the narrow cast-iron pillars of the façade, thus avoiding the need for gutters *per se.*

Encouraged by the success of his experiment Paxton went on to use this new style of framework for conservatory walls and lean-to greenhouses in kitchen and fruit gardens. The design provided maximum light penetra-tion and unusual depth as no intermediary supports were needed thanks to the rigidity of the system. Moreover, the fact that the components could be prefabricated and were easy to install compensated for the additional cost of the glass. The ridge and furrow system proved so effective that Paxton used the concept as the basis for the immensely successful Crystal Palace.[27] In 1836 he again used the system in an innovatory way – to cover the laminat-ed wooden arches of Chatsworth's Great Conservatory, which was built to house tropical plants. The design of the building was completely revolutionary: Paxton adopted a basilica form of exceptional size with a double row of hollow cast-iron columns supporting a cloister arch vault shored up by a half cradle vault going down to ground level. It was a grandiose undertaking and, after its inauguration in 1841, attracted many foreign visitors, including the landscape gardener Pierre Boitard, who the following year came from Paris specifically to see it. He reported that "discerning taste has been applied in the planting of this marvellous garden. On entering the Conservatory by the north door and continuing down the main aisle one sees a succession of different plants – to the right a stand of orange trees, also *Agave americana, Begonia pentaphylla, Dracaena arborea* and *Latania rubra...*, to the left is a rockery planted with ferns and *Ficus repens*, and below one rock a pond framed with stalactites and edged with *Caladium odorum, Cyperus papyrus* and *Nymphaeaceae*; the whole of the central aisle is edged with *Musa paradisiaca* some ten metres in height, *Musa sapientum* and finally, to the south-west is a thicket of fine specimens of *Musa cavendishii* from one of which almost three hundred fruits are hanging this year".[28] Unfortunately cold and humidity proved fatal to this "plant palace",

Bois de Boulogne
Paris
Bagatelle gardens
Orangery, 1844
south façade

as Boitard describes it. To maintain the temperature required by the tropical plants boilers installed below ground had to be fed day and night by small trucks of coal constantly moving along the galleries, which were also built underground. In 1918 the Great Conservatory had to be demolished as it had been left unheated during the war, the woodwork had become rotten, and the plants were in a pitiful state. Space and light were obviously not the only qualities required in a conservatory. From the beginning of the nineteenth century efficient heating systems became increasingly necessary as a structure built of iron and glass was liable to much greater heat loss than a building with a brick façade and traditional roof.

The heating system using hot air pipes below ground or behind the north wall was far from adequate. On the one hand it required an enormous amount of peat or coal to feed it, and on the other it only needed the masonry joints to be less than airtight for sulphur dioxide and carbon monoxide fumes to enter and harm the plants. To rectify some of these problems steam heating systems were introduced shortly after the introduction of the Boulton and Watt engines in 1778, but the system was soon abandoned as boiler explosions were all too frequent. In 1775 the French physician Bonnemain demonstrated his "Principle for heating by water circulation" at the Académie des Sciences; this was based on the convective effect of variation in water density in relation to temperature. However, it was not until 1826, and William Atkinson, that a low-pressure boiler and cast-iron pipe system was finally installed in a greenhouse. The pipes were laid either along the windows or in channels. Three years later Thomas Fowler filed a patent for a siphon to improve water circulation, a system perfected in the 1830s by Angier March Perkins with the high-pressure boiler, which increased the thermal capacity of the system still further.[29]

It now became possible to choose from a wide variety of greenhouses and conservatories capable of meeting every possible requirement in terms of operation and design. Paxton and Loudon were instrumental in encouraging this popularity through the publication of their magazines. In 1834 Paxton launched *Paxton's Magazine of Botany*, and in 1841 *The Gardener's Chronicle*. The articles published in *The Gardener's Magazine*, which Loudon founded in 1826, were already widely read among the middle classes.[30] However, although they paid keen attention to Loudon's advice on gardening it was not until the second half of the century that their real interest in greenhouses began and they started to install the prefabricated structures available from catalogues issued by the major foundries.

By contrast the new owners of the great estates, financiers and industrialists for the most part, showed themselves to be both champions of the new technology – Paxton was their preferred architect – and upholders of a tradition which was in fact altogether foreign to them. They adopted the most modern systems for their kitchen gardens but were even more tempted by conservatories built as traditional extensions to the drawing rooms or libraries of their stately homes. Their new houses were rebuilt in a deliberately traditional neo-Tudor or neo-Elizabethan style and were a somewhat ostentatious reflection of a society which would soon have control over two-thirds of the world. These were immense projects in which the conservatory appears to be no more than an additional part of the decor. In the articles he published between 1829 and 1842 on the great stately homes of England, Loudon acknowledges that the principal and almost sole quality of the conservatory was its ornamental character.[31]

And yet, although the materials used and the design of the conservatory façade were in keeping with the overall architecture of the house, the windows and glass roof (a dome was used at Broughton Hall and Somerleyton and a semicircular vault at Flintham Hall) struck an unusual note which made the conservatory stand out from the rest of the building. It was as if the rather sombre and chilly manor house were there only to set off this new addition, now much more than a mere accessory. The conservatory was a warm and intimate place, filled with light and perfumed with the scent of gardenias, jasmines, roses, and climbers. It was a place unaffected by time or by the seasons, a "paradise lost", the setting for the poets' vain illusion – the eternal idyll of Man and Nature.

However, it would not be long before France too succumbed to its charms and the conservatory was once again transformed, this time into the somewhat strange world of the winter garden. It features in the literature of the period and is described by Balzac as "an architectural gem";[32] by Zola as "a voluptuous greenhouse", a place of temptation to which the heroine of his novel *La Curée* brings her lover only "on those days when her need was for a more intense pleasure"; and for Prince Djalma, the mysterious character in Eugène Sue's novel *The Wandering Jew,* it was a place where the mysteries of India could be recaptured below Parisian skies...

In France the Traditional Meets with the New

Under the Empress Josephine La Malmaison entered a period of ostentatious splendour. During this period the court painter, Jean-Baptiste Isabey, designed the grounds for the Emperor Napoleon in an elegant classical style.

The champagne producer Jean-Rémy Moët had commissioned Isabey to redesign the gardens of his house at Epernay and Napoleon had visited him there.

With a delicate touch Isabey placed a seemingly diaphanous orangery at the end of the formal gardens, terminating the view and allowing it to reflect in the ornamental pond as in a mirror. The building's elegant cornices, columns, and latticework window frames betray its real purpose – to provide a picturesque backdrop.

Unlike the wealthy champagne producer, the Empress Josephine was not interested in "imitation greenhouses"; she wanted functional ones to house the rare species she intended to introduce to the estate. One of the largest hot houses in Europe was built on the estate and in 1805 she made it available to the botanists Brisseau de Mirbel and Etienne-Pierre Ventenat, and in 1809 to Aimé Bonpermet. In 1808, in his work *Descriptions des nouveaux jardins de France*, Alexandre de Laborde describes the estate as the only "genuine botanical garden in France".

The Empress Josephine had a keen interest in botany and was passionate about flowers. Perhaps sensing the precarious future of her gardens – which shortly after her death in 1814 ceased to be maintained – she commissioned the painter Pierre Joseph Redouté to make a permanent record of the plants contained there.

When, in 1802, Redouté accepted the post of "flower painter" at the court he was working for the natural history museum and collaborating with the botanist Alire Raffeneau-Delile, one of the scientists on the Egypt expedition, on the work *Flore d'Egypte*. Redouté made a record of all the plants on the estate in drawings and hand-finished stipple engravings and in 1803 and 1804 published the magnificent work *Jardins de Malmaison* which was followed, between 1812 and 1817, by *Descriptions des plantes rares cultivées à Malmaison et à Navarre*.

It was only after the death of the Empress Josephine that Redouté devoted himself to the rose, which was the flower the Empress had favoured above all others. In the collections *Les Roses* and *Choix des plus belles fleurs*, he illustrates some of the two hundred and fifty varieties grown in Josephine's gardens, many with evocative names such as 'Belle Hébé', 'Beauté Touchante' and 'Parure des Vierges'.

Epernay, Moët et Chandon Estate
Champagne
Jean-Baptiste Isabey
Gardens of the Trianon Residence
Orangery, 1807

BELOW AND FACING PAGE ABOVE:
terracotta medallion busts
FACING PAGE BELOW:
general view
LEFT:
decoration in wood latticework

Pierre Joseph Redouté
Choix des plus belles fleurs, 1827–1833

Left:
Rose of Bengal and White Tea Rose
Below:
Hellebore and Carnation
Facing page above:
Rose, Anemone and Clematis

RIGHT:
La Malmaison Estate
Ile-de-France
design by Jean-Marie Morel, executed by
Jean-Thomas Thibault and Barthélémy
Vignon
Hot houses, 1803–1805
aquatint from a watercolour by Auguste Garneray

In England the First Conservatories are Built

The architects John Nash and Charles Fowler were among the first to realize the new possibilities offered by cast iron and proved themselves adept at making it an integral part of their formal vocabulary.

In 1806 John Nash was commissioned by Sir James Musgrave to build a new conservatory to grace the gardens of the imposing house built at Barnsley Park in 1720 by John Price. Nash decided to complement the grand Italianate residence with its heavy Corinthian pilasters by adding a compatible structure in the Greek style. Cast-iron roof trusses inside the conservatory support sliding sashes and the strengthening rings on the pediments are treated as circular windows that pivot open to provide ventilation. The structure is so light and transparent that it seems to disappear behind the elegant Ionic colonnade of the peripteral temple chosen by Nash as a model. He used a similar design in 1810 at Witley Court for the conservatory commissioned by Lord Foley and in 1820 for the conservatory in the royal gardens at Buckingham Palace.

Nash, in common with many of his fellow architects, was quick to draw on new sources, and found an unexplored repertoire available in the numerous works being published on Ancient Greece. Architects marvelled at the plates in the sumptuous volumes of *The Antiquities of Athens* by James Stuart and Nicholas Revett, the first of which had appeared in 1762 and the fourth in 1816. And the creation in 1803 of the Athenian Society for the study of the most perfect art promoted Philhellenism still further.

In 1820, the young architect and co-founder of the Royal Institute of British Architects, Charles Fowler, was commissioned to build a Great Conservatory on the Duke of Northumberland's Syon Park estate. And in spite of the general infatuation with Ancient Greece it was to Italy that he turned for inspiration.

Barnsley Park
West Yorkshire
John Nash
Conservatory, 1806

FACING PAGE:
east façade, detail
ABOVE:
general view
RIGHT:
detail of corner columns

The gardens of Syon Park, running along the banks of the river Thames near London, had been famous for their rare species since William Turner, a doctor, had created England's first botanical garden there in 1545.

This was lost between 1767 and 1773 when Capability Brown landscaped the grounds but Turner's garden had left an indelible impression and Fowler decided to re-create it, if only in spirit. Fowler went for inspiration to *I Quattro Libri dell'Architettura* by Andrea Palladio and took as his model the unfinished villa of Counts Lodovico and Francesco Trissino at Meledo. This building with its semicircular plan was highly reminiscent of the Veneto and the Horto dei Medici at Padua, forerunners, along with the garden at Pisa, of all botanical gardens.

Unlike Nash, for whom the new techniques available were merely a means of refining his model, Fowler used Palladian influences to treat the conservatory in an entirely modern way. The dome over the central section of the Trissino villa provided him with the opportunity to apply the new theories on curvilinear greenhouses. The conservatory façades were built of golden Bath stone, contrasting with the ornate cast-iron structure of the interior supporting a cupola that appears to float on air.

Fowler's contemporaries were particularly impressed by this dome, which was the first of its type to be built in England. It was constructed entirely of cast iron, from the drum to the ribs – only the strengthening rings were made of wrought iron – and given added stability and rigidity through its parabolic profile and the customary overlapping panes of glass.

However, few recognized the ethereal quality Fowler had given Palladio's villa, whose long *barchesse*, terminating in porticos, are marvellously reproduced in the two wings of the conservatory with its elegant curves.

Claudius Loudon himself, writing in 1833, declared that the simplicity and grandeur of the Ionic style of conservatory far surpassed that used at Syon Park, and was the most beautiful of its kind in England.

Syon Park
London
Charles Fowler
Great Conservatory, 1820–1827

ABOVE AND
FACING PAGE BELOW:
details of the corner pavilions
LEFT:
general view

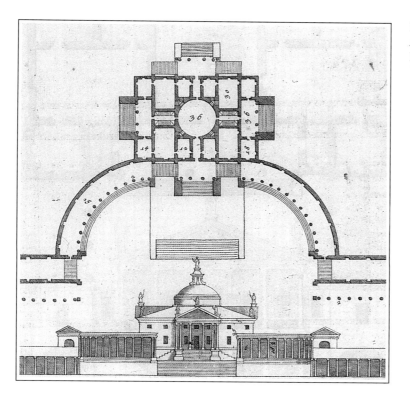

LEFT:
Andrea Palladio
I Quattro Libri dell'Architettura, 1570
Villa Trissino at Meledo

Syon Park
London
Charles Fowler
Great Conservatory, 1820–1827

ABOVE:
interior view, side wing
FACING PAGE:
interior view, central rotunda

The Conservatory Redefined

The architect Jeffry Wyatville received many prestigious commissions from 1800 onwards but even the more modest commission to build a conservatory was greeted with a fresh and original response. When building Wyatville's main concern was always the quality of the construction rather than its appearance, and he paid scant regard to ornamentation or styles.

He applied the same basic principles to the first conservatory he built – at Longleat – that he would later apply at Belton House, Wilton House, Chatsworth, and the Royal Gardens at Kew. The masonry shell is reduced to simple pilasters in very light relief, which hold the tall guillotine sashes of the façades, except on the north side which, as was the custom, is left blind. Wyatville's sole concession to tradition is to crown the cornice with a balustrade or ornament it with vases to conceal the glass roof, this giving the profile of an orangery.

In 1815 he built the conservatory at Belton House, and this gave him the opportunity to display his ingenuity to the full. By using a double structure – masonry for the shell, filiform columns and a cast-iron frame on the interior – he "opened up" the roof and increased the internal space of the conservatory to meet the increasing demand for varieties of palm and banana trees.

Wyatville became the expert in this type of structure; in 1824 he received a commission from the Duke of Devonshire for a glasshouse at Chatsworth and two years later another from Lord Pembroke for his Wilton House estate. At Wilton House he reinitiated a project conceived by his uncle James Wyatt when he was extending the house between 1801 and 1811. However, he did not succeed in re-creating the elegant architecture his uncle had produced, nor did he manage to repeat the astonishing interior space he had at Belton House.

In 1836 he converted the conservatory built by John Nash for the gardens of Buckingham Palace and later moved to Kew, where it became known as the Exotic House.

ABOVE:
Wilton House
Wiltshire
stone seat, c. 1730

LEFT:
Kew Gardens
London
John Nash and Jeffry Wyatville
Exotic House (now *Aroid House*), 1825–1836

LEFT:
Wilton House
Wiltshire
James Wyatt and Jeffry Wyatville
Conservatory, c. 1811–1826

RIGHT:
Belton House
Lincolnshire
Jeffry Wyatville
Conservatory, 1815

Belton House
Lincolnshire
Jeffry Wyatville
Conservatory, 1815

LEFT, BELOW AND FACING PAGE ABOVE:
interior views

Belton House
Lincolnshire
Jeffry Wyatville
Conservatory, 1815

Right:
odalisque in niche

Camellia Houses

The camellia was sent back from China at the end of the seventeenth century by Georg Josef Kamel, a Jesuit looking for tea plants. However, it did not bloom in the west until 1739, at Thorndon Hall. In 1646 it had been given the name *Rosa sinensis* by the priest Giovanni Battista Ferrari but the species in fact came from Japan and Korea, and was renamed *Camellia japonica* by Linné.

At the beginning of the nineteenth century the camellia became all the rage, with horticulturists succeeding in identifying some fifty different varieties. Many plant lovers now kept a camellia house. The camellia was popular because it bloomed early in the year and was highly attractive, its dark, glistening foliage providing the perfect foil to the delicate flowers in every shade from the purest white to the richest red. But for Marie Duplessis, the inspiration for *La Dame aux camélias*, it was their one failing, their lack of fragrance, that made them attractive.

In 1823 Lord Middleton placed an order with the Birmingham firm Thomas Clarke to build a vast conservatory in the gardens of Wollaton Hall to house his delicate camellias, which were unable to tolerate either frost or extreme heat. As the camellia does not require much light the roof was constructed in alternating sections of copper and glass. The whole structure is supported on gutter beams and slender, hollow cast-iron columns. Metal is also used on the façade: cast iron for the engaged columns and the architrave, lead for the vases protruding from the cornice and copper for the window frames.

The conservatory at Wollaton Hall was a totally new concept: it was the first building to be constructed from components prefabricated in a factory. Despite the advantages of the system it was not an example that was widely followed, although two years later Charles Robert Cockerell did ask the same firm to produce an identical building to be installed on the Grange estate. It was not until the Great Exhibition of 1851 and the construction of the Crystal Palace that the prefabricated conservatory began to appear in catalogues of cast-iron structures for the garden and finally became fashionable.

Wollaton Hall
Nottinghamshire
Camellia House, 1823

FACING PAGE ABOVE:
centre aisle
FACING PAGE BELOW:
general view
RIGHT:
entrance detail
BELOW:
view of vaulting and ribbed segments

Pierre Joseph Redouté
Choix des plus belles fleurs, 1827–1833

LEFT:
White Camellia
BELOW:
Variegated Camellia
FACING PAGE ABOVE:
Anemone-flowered Camellia

RIGHT:
Bretton Hall
Yorkshire
Jeffry Wyatville
Camelia House, 1816
corner pavilion

Paxton and the Conservatory Wall

Following his initial experiment on the old orangery at Chatsworth, between 1828 and 1850 Paxton began to produce greenhouses and conservatories with ridge and furrow roofs. Of the buildings he constructed on the estate only a conservatory wall still remains, unfortunately without its original roof. In 1848, along a 100 m (330 ft) length of wall Paxton built a narrow, glass shelter with removable wooden frames in which espalier vines, peaches, and fig trees could be grown protected from the elements. Although the famous roofing system has disappeared this nevertheless remains a structure of great elegance. Paxton varied the structure by creating a series of pavilions, "breaking up" the façade and highlighting each section with a frieze of cast-iron palmettes.

Following the success of the Crystal Palace at the Great Exhibition of 1851 many landowners approached Paxton to build hot houses in a variety of styles and for a variety of purposes.

His reputation quickly grew and several members of the Rothschild banking family living in London, Paris, and Geneva commissioned him not only to lay out their gardens but also to build their residences. As an architect Paxton remained traditional, adhering to the neo-classical style fashionable at the time. However, he demonstrated his expertise to the full in the many greenhouses he designed and built between 1857 and 1859 in the gardens of Baron James de Rothschild at Ferrières near Paris. These included houses for aroids, orchids, and aquatic plants and also an unheated greenhouse for the container-grown shrubs which decorated the formal gardens in the summer months.

Of the buildings constructed by Paxton for the Rothschild family only the delightful orangery-aviary dating from the 1860s still remains; this was created to a design by Paxton or his son-in-law George H. Stokes at the request of Baron Adolphe de Rothschild for his property at Pregny, overlooking Geneva and the lake.

Chatsworth
Derbyshire
Joseph Paxton
Conservatory wall, 1848

FACING PAGE:
central pavilion
ABOVE:
transverse view

RIGHT:
Château de Pregny
Geneva
orangery and aviary, 1860–1870
general view

In England Paxton's new clientele were mainly among the increasing number of industrialists and financiers acquiring the estates of impoverished country squires and rebuilding the houses with a splendour that was impressive but often short-lived.

One of these was Sir Morton Peto, a fabulously wealthy railway constructor, who built railways in Great Britain and also in Russia, Canada, and Argentina. In 1843 he acquired the Somerleyton estate near the small port of Lowestoft on the North Sea coast and in 1851, once his architect, John Thomas, had finished rebuilding the old Elizabethan manor house, the industrialist commissioned Paxton to lay out an enormous kitchen garden.

This was a delightful walled garden where fruit trees could grow protected from the north winds by the high walls. On two sides Paxton built conservatory walls; the one at the entrance housed peaches, the other, which was a good deal larger and along the north wall, was originally used for growing vines. Today this is the only example that remains of Paxton's ridge and furrow system; it has cast-iron gutter joists strengthened by truss rods to free the interior of any load-bearing elements.

It is interesting to note that Paxton departs from his normal practice and uses metal not wood for the structural frame, no doubt at his client's request, but he reverts to wood for the window frames.

Somerleyton Hall
Suffolk
Joseph Paxton
*conservatory wall enclosing
the fruit garden on the south side*, c. 1850

ABOVE:
porch
LEFT:
main gate
FACING PAGE:
side wing

Somerleyton Hall
Suffolk
Joseph Paxton
*conservatory wall enclosing
the fruit garden on the north side*, c. 1850

LEFT:
façade, detail

Somerleyton Hall
Suffolk
Joseph Paxton
*conservatory wall enclosing
the fruit garden on the north side,*
c. 1850

Right:
general view
Above and facing page below:
interior views

Stately Homes and Garden Rooms

By the 1830s architects were choosing to make the conservatory an integral part of the design of the new stately houses commissioned by owners who wanted to see their newly acquired estates returned to their former glory. These vast residences, built in a neo-Tudor or neo-Elizabethan style, with turrets, oriel windows, and projecting bays, could happily incorporate a garden room.

At Mamhead House Anthony Salvin designed the conservatory in the style of a neo-Gothic chapel with diagonal arch windows, door frames in enamelled cast iron and a belvedere giving a view of the sea in the distance. At Harlaxton Manor, however, a different approach was taken. In 1838 William Burn was asked to complete the work that had been started by Salvin, and decided to create the more unusual atmosphere of a nymphs' grotto.

The estate had been acquired in the fifteenth century by a branch of the Ligne family, who had fled to England from Flanders to escape religious persecution. In 1831 the last descendant of the family, a businessman by the name of Gregory Gregory, had the old manor house razed to the ground. His wish was to emulate his ancestor the Prince de Ligne, the renowned owner of the Belœil gardens. Burn was inspired by this to create an unconventional design for the conservatory interior. The conservatory is entered via a high doorway, guarded on either side by terms on pillars. This leads to a rotunda of mysterious charm, which serves simply as an antechamber to the sumptuous gardens with their grotto, fountains, and multiple terraces rising up behind the house.

Despite their owners' fanciful ideas the conservatories at Mamhead House, Harlaxton Manor, and Stoke Rocheford were built in a tradition that did not disturb or challenge the design of the main building. The same is not true at Broughton Hall, Avington Park, and Flintham Hall. On these estates the conservatories were built as part of the remodelling or extension work on the existing buildings and this gave the architects the opportunity to liberate themselves from the general style and choose freely the method of construction and the materials they wished to use.

Left:
Stoke Rocheford
Lincolnshire
William Burn
Conservatory, c. 1845
general view

LEFT:
Harlaxton Manor
Lincolnshire
William Burn
Conservatory, 1838
general view

Mamhead House
Devon
Anthony Salvin
Conservatory, 1830

RIGHT:
general view
FACING PAGE ABOVE:
south façade

The two Leeds architects working at Broughton Hall knew exactly what it was possible to achieve with the use of cast iron and created a wonderful, light-filled conservatory that blended well with the existing house. Broughton Hall was originally built in the sixteenth century but had been constantly enlarged and updated in line with the fashions of the period. In 1839 George Webster decorated the north façade with a Palladian portico of immense proportions. Later the owner, Sir Charles Tempest, an aesthete and lover of rare flowers, commissioned Andrews and Delaunay to design a new conservatory to match the neo-Palladian style of the Hall but which would also meet the technical requirements and provide the plants with sufficient light and heat.

In North Yorkshire the sun shines only too rarely and the architects therefore decided to create an "indoor garden" beyond the billiard room, thus ensuring that three of the four façades would be external. To further increase the available light, and to ensure adequate ventilation, the cast-iron trusses of the framework were fitted with brackets and ornate ridge sheets supporting a raised glass roof with opening panels. However, by way of contrast they completed the structure with a very Palladian touch, terminating the long central aisle in a rotunda crowned by a transparent dome that relieved the austerity of the design. This feature, which emphasizes the classical style of the façades, combines delightfully with the Italian-style gardens that surround the conservatory. The gardens with their balustraded terraces, and beds with box hedging, were laid out by the landscape designer William Andrews Nesfield and indicate a return to the Renaissance-style garden.

The owner of Avington Park also took advantage of the new possibilities offered by the use of cast iron. In fact, in 1851, following the success of the Great Exhibition in London, Sir John Shelly became one of the first to purchase a prefabricated conservatory for the manor house he had acquired three years earlier. This was composed entirely of manufactured units that were assembled on site, and was the forerunner of the verandas and winter gardens that would soon appear on the market. As was the case with the latter, the conservatory's main function was no longer the protection of tender plants; it was on its way to becoming an attractive garden accessory.

Broughton Hall
North Yorkshire
Andrews and Delaunay
Conservatory, 1853

Above and facing page:
general view of conservatory and gardens
designed by William Andrews Nesfield
Left:
rotunda dome

Broughton Hall
North Yorkshire
Andrews and Delaunay
Conservatory, 1853

LEFT:
glass roof above the central aisle
BELOW:
interior

Broughton Hall
North Yorkshire
Andrews and Delaunay
Conservatory, 1853

Above:
cupola and main aisle
Right:
capital on hollow pillars

Today only two side pavilions remain, attached to the façade facing the park. These elegant structures provided Lord Shelly with additional space and a new environment in which to hold the extravagant festivities, for which the estate had been famous since the beginning of the century. Every year, in May, magnificent receptions were held in honour of the Prince Regent, later to become George IV, and the beautiful Mrs Fitzherbert, and the wooden orangery, which had stood on the site of the new conservatory, was transformed into a veritable "Flora's palace".

The Great Exhibition created a vogue for modernization and Flintham Hall was no exception to this trend; however, the modernization work at the Hall did not hinder the development of a poetical ambience in the building. The Hall was restored in 1850 in the style of an Italian palace, and three years later a conservatory extension was added. The size of the structure and the metal-framed barrel vault are a clear demonstration of the attraction that the Crystal Palace had for architects generally, and the Avington Hall architect, T. C. Hine, in particular.

However, any similarity was only superficial. Lord T. B. Thoroton Hildyard, the owner of the estate, was enthralled by the nostalgic visions of the first Pre-Raphaelite poets and painters and wanted to re-create the disturbing and even mysterious atmosphere of a Florentine palace. Among the beds of jasmine and amaryllis water spills from a marble fountain brought back from Tuscany, and, at sunset, tall, narrow, round-headed windows give a view of the trees at a nearby church.

Above the elegant arcade opening on to the vast and sombre library a voice appears to arise from a small loggia overlooking the winter garden, engulfed in the shades of evening, and murmur the lines of Dante Gabriel Rossetti:

> The blessèd Damozel lean'd out
> From the gold bar of Heaven:
> Her blue grave eyes were deeper much
> Than a deep water, even.
> She had three lilies in her hand,
> And the stars in her hair were seven.

Avington Park
Hampshire
Conservatory, 1850

FACING PAGE:
connecting gallery
ABOVE:
detail of side pavilion
RIGHT:
general view

Flintham Hall
Nottinghamshire
T.C. Hine
Conservatory, 1853–1854

ABOVE:
view from below
LEFT:
general view
FACING PAGE:
window interior

5

FINAL SPLENDOUR

The unbridled triumph of allusion

"Faced with the harsh daily reality of the profit motive... art will take on a compensatory role, escape into the past being a characteristic feature of this: escape into the past, into the world of fantasy, into myth...".[1]

By the 1830s the architect had entered the world of escapism, using different methods and exploring different influences, and so too did the landscape gardener. Garden design had become monotonous, and, though it may have blended harmoniously, it had been stuck in a rut since the end of the previous century. For the landscape gardener too, revisiting the past became a means of escape.

Humphry Repton had already realized that over-dependence on the pictorial arts was bound to lead to an impasse. He reiterated the importance of the role played by movement in the perception of space; the temptation to create a landscape in the style of Claude Lorraine or Salvator Rosa had become so great that the question of movement had been all too easily forgotten. And yet, as Repton explained, a gardener surveys the landscape while walking, whereas for the painter the place from which the view is seen is fixed.[2] John Claudius Loudon attempted to introduce a new, temporal dimension into his work. For the landscape gardener Nature was a raw material which needed to be embellished by Art.[3] It could therefore no longer serve as a model itself and the artist was obliged to find other sources of inspiration. This prompted a fresh interest in the historical, manifested through the numerous creations of the past. However, unlike in the previous century, this was no longer simply a matter of installing structures of ancient or medieval design to inspire noble sentiments; the whole composition, both the residence and the gardens, must be designed to evoke the historical. In 1822, after a journey around Europe Loudon published his *Encyclopaedia of Gardening*. This was the first history of landscape gardening to appear and served as a splendid reference work for his contemporaries.[4]

Before the influence of Italy and France again began to dominate, it was the Orient that became a source of inspiration for designers, enabling them to introduce into their compositions the new dimension that was sorely lacking. The conservatory with its exotic plants, glass domes, and the ornamental possibilities of its cast ironwork, lent itself to this better than any other structure and it became the garden "accessory" of choice.

During the 1790s India became a source of fascination. Following Clive's victory in 1757 at the battle of Plassey, which gave them control of Bengal, the East India Company had pursued a policy of territorial annexation, reinforced a century later by the appointment of a viceroy of India.[5] To provide scientific grounds for its military and commercial activities the powerful East India Company encouraged research into the flora and fauna not only of Bengal but also of Burma and Nepal. At the suggestion of Colonel Robert Kyd the Company had been involved in the creation of a botanical garden in Calcutta and this in turn led to the publication, between 1795 and 1819, of the splendid volumes entitled *Plants of the Coast of Coromandel*, also under the auspices of the Company. This work, which enabled an eager public to see for itself the marvellous flora of India, was produced by the garden's first curator, William Roxburgh, and published with the collaboration of Sir Joseph Banks, director of the Royal Botanic Gardens, Kew. This was followed in 1832 by *Plantae asiaticae rariores*, again published with the support of the East India Company, and it was here that Nathaniel Wallich, Roxburgh's successor, produced the first illustration of *Amherstia nobilis*, an extremely rare tree from Burma whose long blooms hanging in clusters of scarlet were used as an offering to the gods.[6]

Not only the flora of India but also her architecture fascinated the British. The architect Samuel Pepys Cockerell was impressed by the scenes Thomas Daniell had painted in *A Picturesque "Voyage" to India* and used them as inspiration to build a spectacular Moghul palace at Sezincote, on the Gloucestershire estate of his brothers John and Charles Cockerell, retired officers of the East India Company. The palace had an adjoining conservatory, in the style of the verandas of India, and a strange but charming garden designed by Daniell with the assistance of Humphry Repton.[7]

Just as the marvels of India were a continued source of fascination for the Cockerell brothers, many aristocrats and industrialists found themselves captivated by the delights of the Orient. Their fascination was not simply an expression of nostalgia for places they had visited or the appetite for the unusual that had characterized the previous century; they felt the need to appropriate for themselves the delights of lands, which, although controlled by them, still remained entirely alien and exotic.

The whole of the Orient, from Arabia to China, became fashionable, and, on estates such as Somerleyton and Alton Towers, provided the inspiration for enchanting new buildings and gardens – not least of which was the conservatory – and also for the most outrageous eccentricities.

On the Continent William I, King of Württemberg, shared the same fascination and in 1836 commissioned Karl Ludwig von Zanth to build him a new summer residence, known as La Wilhelma, on a hill in the Rosenstein park, near Stuttgart. Although the King did not ask his architect to follow a specific model he did indicate the atmosphere he wished to achieve in the description of the project, which was to be "a residence and ornamental glasshouses in the Moorish style".[8]

Around 1820, Zanth became inspired by the architecture of the Umayyad caliphs of Andalusia. An early study of Moorish architecture by James Cavanah Murphy – *The Arabian Antiquities of Spain* – published in 1813, had introduced him to the splendours of the Alhambra palace in Granada. From the outset, Zanth treated his new commission as an exercise in style, drawing on the rich ornamental repertoire of Muslim architecture. Work on La Wilhelma did not begin in full until 1842 and was completed in 1854. During the course of construction an even more valuable source became available to Zanth: in 1848 the architect Owen Jones published detailed drawings of the Alhambra under the title *Alhambra, Plans, Elevations, Sections and Details*.[9] Zanth's research into polychromy and his refinement of detail enabled him to satisfy his client's requirements while still managing to retain complete freedom in what was a highly personal interpretation.

Zanth's approach was a purely rational one; he did not share the view of his compatriot Friedrich von Schlegel, an ardent champion of German Romantic thought, that "it is to the Orient that we must turn for the supreme expression of Romanticism".[10] Zanth's interpretation was considered too intellectual and received an unenthusiastic response from his royal clients, who were enthralled by the exotic lifestyle of the sultans and pashas. It needed the skill of a theatrical designer to re-create the enchantment of the Orient and this was where Karl Friedrich Schinkel came in. Schinkel, who was already renowned for the sets he had created for Schiller's *The Maid of Orleans*, understood perfectly what was needed and in 1829 created a palm house in the gardens of the residence of King Frederick William III of Prussia, on the Pfaueninsel or Peacock Island. Behind the tall neo-classical façade Schinkel decorated the cast-iron structure of the building with copies of statues in marble, silk hangings, and latticework screens worthy of the palace in the *Arabian Nights*. All that now remains of this marvellous interior are the wonderful canvases by Karl Blechen, as the building was destroyed by fire in 1880.

Others were tempted to seek the "supreme expression of Romanticism" by escaping to a more fantastical past – the era of knights and troubadours. From 1830 onwards France and Central Europe followed the example of England and "erected churches and stately homes throughout the land in numbers quite astonishing at a period of industrial development such as this".[11] Many of these enormous houses were remodelled in the Tudor style as this appeared to lend itself best to re-creating the atmosphere of a fantastical medieval past. However, the sultry air and filtered light of the oriental palace was much better suited to the conservatory than to the cold severity of castle rooms. And often, as at the Schwarzenberg palace in Bohemia, this re-creation of the past was limited to a purely ornamental likeness.

Following a visit to England for the coronation of Queen Victoria, Prince Jan Adolf II of Schwarzenberg had the old Hlubokà fortress, overlooking the Vltava river, transformed into a Tudor-style manor house. Between 1845 and 1847 the architect, Franz Beer, built a conservatory that connected the house with the manège. This was a veritable cathedral of glass with scalloped tracery and cast-iron pinnacles, a neo-Gothic concoction attached to an entirely separate building. Perhaps only one project was entirely successful in expressing the Romantic dream of both client and architect and this was the Margheria, a model farm built on the Racconigi estate near Turin for the King of Sardinia by the architect Pelagio Palagi.[12] The Margheria was interpreted in the medieval style and consisted of farm buildings, a greenhouse, and gardens. However, both Palagi and the King were blind to the impending economic crisis that would soon shake the Piedmont region.

It was not long before architects and landscape gardeners started to realize that escapism into oriental fantasy or historical styles was simply an illusion. In a vain attempt to halt the passage of time, and with it the acceleration of urban expansion and industrial progress, they turned to the unchanging serenity of the Mediterranean countryside for inspiration. They combined the influence of Ancient Rome with their personal impressions, gleaned from their travels, and rediscovered the forgotten charms of the gardens of the Renaissance with their avenues of cypress trees and gardens of orange trees. They also found new charm in the farmhouses or *cascine* scattered about the Roman countryside.[13] The value they placed on this type of architecture provided a new raison d'être and the orangery gave them the opportunity to recapture the yearned-for vision of a golden age. The Garden of the Hesperides in the form of the orangery returned once more to the repertoire of architects who had abandoned it, to be re-created, with additions, in a highly classical style.

At this time the orangery underwent a brief renaissance in many areas of Europe: in France, as we have already seen, in the Bagatelle gardens and those of the Tuileries, at Wrest Park in England, and at the royal residences of Würtzburg and Potsdam in Germany. The ageless architecture of the orangery and the "secret gardens" that were often created around it seemed to fix space in time. However, the orangery no longer served any real purpose, the prestige attached to it was a thing of the past, and this brief revival was soon over. But before this happened one last royal dream was fulfilled: King Frederick William IV of Prussia built an orangery in the gardens of his Sans-Souci residence at Potsdam that combined the features of both the Bramante Belvedere and the Medici Villa.

Historically the orangery's development was marked by ever greater splendour, yet now it stands empty, and orange and pomegranate trees no longer line the edges of lawns. The orangery has lost not only its vocation but also its identity: what was once an orangery has now become a concert room or exhibition hall – or simply the tea room in a public park.

Edouard Muller
The Garden of Armida, 1855
wallpaper by the Desfossé company, Paris

Nostalgia or the Exercise in Style

When John Cockerell returned to England after years in Bengal it was with a single dream: to recreate on the estate of Sezincote purchased in 1795, the style of the palaces he had so admired in India.

However, it was for his brother Charles that Samuel Pepys Cockerell, the youngest member of the family, designed an Indian villa with a long adjoining conservatory-veranda. Inspiration came from the residences of the Moghul princes, juxtaposing the "peacock-tail" arcature of the windows, characteristic of Rajasthan, with Muslim features such as *chattris* – small minarets adorning the roof – and Persian features such as the bulb-shaped central dome.

The adjoining gardens reveal other curious aspects of India. Dominating the whole is the temple of the goddess Surya; down in a small valley a portico inspired by the entrance to the Elephanta caves stands submerged beneath lush vegetation.

Cockerell, as architect, and Thomas Daniell and Humphry Repton as designers of the garden, succeeded in creating a splendid harmony between the melancholic appeal of Nature in England and the exuberance of Indian architecture. This was rediscovered in the 1890s by the Indian watercolourist Lehcim Naduas, whose mother was British. Naduas, a friend of Colonel Arthur Dugdale, who owned the estate at the time, returned to India with his sketchbooks and many of the colonel's friends found his views of Sezincote, with their contrasting and yet highly intimate juxtaposition of two different worlds, quite disconcerting.

The Prince Regent, later George IV, had visited Sezincote and been deeply impressed by the villa and gardens in 1806, and soon after he commissioned John Nash to "indianize" the Royal Pavilion at Brighton, a summer residence that had been refurbished in a somewhat unfortunate manner between 1786 and 1804. As the model the architect was following was itself already a copy he was able to give himself a completely free hand.

Brighton
East Sussex
Royal Pavilion, 1787
John Nash
converted in 1818

ABOVE:
central pavilion
LEFT AND FACING PAGE ABOVE:
French windows

BELOW:
Lehcim Naduas
After the storm at Sezincote, 1895
watercolour

Barton Seagrave Hall
Northamptonshire
Conservatory, c. 1820

<small>Left:</small>
glazing with peacock tail motif
<small>Facing page below:</small>
south façade

<small>Below:</small>
Nathaniel Wallich
Plantae asiaticae rariores, 1832
Amherstia nobilis

ABOVE:
William Roxburgh
Plants of the Coast of Coromandel, 1795–1819
Butea frondosa

The same fascination for the exotic – an exotic more fictional than real – inspired Charles Talbot, Earl of Shrewsbury when, between 1814 and 1827, he commissioned Thomas Allason and Robert Abrahams to transform Alveton Lodge, his country house near Alton in Staffordshire. For the main residence the architects chose to follow a neo-Gothic line, though not in a specific style. When in 1831 Loudon visited the property, which was renamed Alton Towers, he remarked that it was the strangest of anomalies to be found among the country houses of England.

The grounds, on the other hand, were treated as an opportunity to evoke the most distant lands and civilizations. Greek temples paid homage to the perfection of Hellenic art, while a reconstruction of Stonehenge celebrated the dawn of architecture. Distant and unfamiliar lands received a more conventional treatment. Down in a steep-sided valley a delightful pond and pagoda could be found; these were inspired by the works of William Chambers, notably his *Dissertation on Oriental Gardening* published in 1772, which included descriptions of China that were much debated.

On a more subtle note the Earl asked for his gardens to be filled with sounds and fragrances evoking fabled times and enchanted places. At the top of a valley lined with terraces of flowers a blind harpist played, reminiscent of Ossian, the Celtic hero revered by the poet James Macpherson. A conservatory with seven glass domes was placed on the other side, fragrant with perfumes from many parts of the globe. In the central section – a hot house for palm trees and bananas – gilded cages of exotic birds were suspended from the cast-iron network of the domes with large pools below them. On either side two open galleries led to the side pavilions, where in winter orange, pomegranate, and bay trees were stored.

No epitaph could have been more fitting for Lord Talbot, this prince of an imaginary Orient, than that inscribed on his mausoleum by his nephew John Talbot – "He made the Desert smile".

Alton Towers
Staffordshire
Thomas Allason and Robert Abrahams
gardens, created 1814–1827

Above:
pagoda
Facing page below:
general view of conservatory

P. Boitard
**Traité de la composition
et de l'ornement des jardins**, 1839

Left:
"Chinese gateway"
Facing page above:
Chinese orangery at the home of Mr Panckoucke

Aumont del.   Durawse sc.

Unknown Japanese artist
Livre de modèles pour s'initier à l'art du dessin, c. 1856

Below:
poppy
Facing page above:
camellia

Alton Towers
Staffordshire
Thomas Allason and Robert Abrahams
Conservatory, 1827

RIGHT:
open gallery
FACING PAGE ABOVE:
side pavilion

Alton Towers
Staffordshire
Thomas Allason and Robert Abrahams
Conservatory, 1827

ABOVE:
cupola detail in the central pavilion
LEFT AND FACING PAGE:
interior and main dome

Bewitchment and Curiosity

Karl Ludwig von Zanth's curiosity for all things ancient made it simple for him to embrace the Moorish style chosen by King William I for his new residence near Stuttgart. Von Zanth remarks, "What I gained from the Arab architects was a vision of unbridled inspiration rather than established principles and constraints".

First Zanth turned to the proven formula of "villas designed in the style of the country houses of the Italian nobility". La Wilhelma was built in this classic style. The residence overlooked the grounds and a vast formal garden with exedra, "an oriental garden" of delicate blooms, magnolias and water lilies in profusion. A covered way running around the perimeter and punctuated at intervals by kiosks in the Ottoman style connected the residence to a reception room.

Zanth embellished this canvas with a wealth of the most fantastical Moorish features. He played with the polychromy of stone, incorporated the horseshoe arch and covered the central pavilion with an enormous Ottoman dome of gilded copper, unfortunately replaced by a glass roof which still mars the overall effect today. The cast-iron construction of the conservatories enabled Zanth to echo the allusion by creating pillars, arches, strengthening rings, grilles, and cornices ornamented in the Arab style.

However, Zanth was not merely a decorator. Recalling the glasshouses of the Paris Muséum d'Histoire Naturelle that he had visited in 1833 when Rohault de Fleury was completing them, he followed his example and gave the conservatory wings cast-iron façades constructed from prefabricated components made in the factory.

A new feature that Zanth introduced, however, was to separate the skeleton and the frames, which were also cast-iron sections, thus preventing the frames from warping under the pressure of the structure. He was therefore able to apply the lightness of touch required for the chosen style, which went well beyond a simple ornamental curiosity.

Karl Ludwig von Zanth
La Wilhelma, 1842–1854
Stuttgart, Baden-Württemberg

ABOVE:
covered gallery with flower border
FACING PAGE:
reception pavilion, 1847–1851

LEFT:
Charles Bélanger
Voyages aux Indes orientales, 1834
houses on the Bosphorus

Karl Ludwig von Zanth
La Wilhelma, 1842–1854
Stuttgart, Baden-Württemberg
Moorish villa and ornamental glasshouses, 1842–1846

FACING PAGE AND ABOVE:
windows on the south façade
RIGHT:
general view

Karl Ludwig von Zanth
La Wilhelma, 1842–1854
Stuttgart, Baden-Württemberg
Ornamental glasshouses, 1842–1846

Above:
side pavilion
corner
FACING PAGE BELOW:
side pavilion
general view

Karl Ludwig von Zanth
La Wilhelma, 1842–1854
Stuttgart, Baden-Württemberg
Ornamental glasshouses, 1842–1846

Right and facing page below:
façade, structural details

A Disconcerting Modernity

In 1840 Duke Alois II, Prince of Liechtenstein, inherited property at Lednice and Valtice in southern Moravia; this was an estate that had been in the family since the thirteenth century and would remain so until its expropriation in 1918.

At first he was content to continue his father's work maintaining the vast park laid out in the English style at the end of the eighteenth century. To prevent the annual flooding of the river Dyje a number of small lakes and streams had been created and in their waters a Roman aqueduct, a minaret, an Ottoman kiosk, and a ruined castle could still be seen reflected.

The young Duke sent his own architect, Georg Wingelmüller, on a trip to England to study its architecture so that on his return the old Baroque palace could be transformed into a magnificent Tudor mansion. This began in 1847 but the scale of the work was such that it was not completed until 1858, by Johann Heidrich.

To build the conservatory, which adjoins the drawing rooms in the English fashion, the Duke sent to Britain for P. H. Devien, an architect specializing in this field. Devien adopted the still somewhat audacious system created by the celebrated architect John Claudius Loudon for the conservatory structure. This consisted of a network of curvilinear semicircular ribs, terminated by a quarter sphere, creating a close grid to hold the panes of glass and giving the structure rigidity and wind resistance.

Devien somewhat unexpectedly complements the entirely functional nature of the structure with an atmosphere more reminiscent of an Ottoman seraglio than a modern greenhouse by filtering the light through the latticework of the frame. A few exotic touches – the pattern of the ventilation grilles borrowed from Persian rug designs and the banana leaf capitals of the cast-iron pillars – give the conservatory the bewitching charm of the oriental gardens there had been a vain attempt to re-create in the grounds during the previous century.

Lednice Palace
Moravia
P.H. Devien
Conservatory, 1847–1848

Above:
cast-iron capital with banana tree motif
Facing page:
interior

Left:
Charles Bélanger
Voyages aux Indes orientales, 1834
Ottoman princesses

Lednice Palace
Moravia
P.H. Devien
Conservatory, 1847–1848

FACING PAGE:
view of main span
ABOVE:
side exit

RIGHT:
Pfaueninsel
Berlin
Karl Friedrich Schinkel
Palmenhaus, 1829–1831
interior
oil painting by Karl Blechen, 1832

Medieval Reveries

During the French Restoration the Racconigi estate, which was confiscated in 1798 by the Bonapartist army, was returned to the house of Savoie-Carignan. The palace had been rebuilt between 1676 and 1681 according to plans drawn up by Guarino Guarini and, during the eighteenth century, was refurbished in the Palladian style. However, the young prince, Carlo-Alberto, did not choose to have the palace remodelled in the medieval style. He dreamt of experimenting with new methods of agriculture, just at the time when the movement of labour from the countryside to the towns to work in industry had already begun.

The prince became King of Sardinia in 1831 and enlarged the estate. He commissioned Pelagio Palagi to design a model farm, the Margheria, which was completed in 1834.

In line with Palagi's Romanesque vision his disciple Carlo Sada built an enormous hot house to complete the complex. This was both a *limonaia* and conservatory, retaining the internal features of the former with its pointed barrel vault, where container-grown plants could be housed. From the conservatory it borrowed the fully glazed façade and the wall base frames for fragile fruits such as peaches, melons, and pineapples. As a finishing touch Burdin, a nurseryman from Turin, was commissioned to import from England rare species still unknown at that period such as the famous *Magnolia grandiflora*, the *Sophora japonica*, the tulip tree, and the ginkgo, now found on the great Piedmont estates.

The model farm was abandoned in 1848 when the king was exiled; he had been so absorbed in his utopian dream that he had been unaware of the economic crisis facing the Piedmont region.

Today the Margheria is but a melancholy reflection of an impossible dream, a mirage liable to vanish for ever, forgotten by all.

Racconigi Palace
Piedmont, Italy
La Margheria, 1834–1836
Carlo Sada
glasshouse, 1836

FACING PAGE ABOVE:
side and front façades
FACING PAGE BELOW:
Pelagio Palagi
farm buildings
LEFT:
general view from the park
BELOW:
interior

Hlubokà Palace
Bohemia
Franz Beer
Conservatory, 1845–1847

FACING PAGE:
façade detail
ABOVE:
main entrance
RIGHT:
general view

Arcadia Rediscovered

The young landscape gardener Peter Joseph Lenné arrived in Berlin in 1816 at a time when the Prussian capital was still celebrating the end of the Napoleonic saga and the court was again beginning to show interest in enlarging its palaces and gardens.

Lenné's association with the court architect Karl Friedrich Schinkel resulted in him distancing himself from the sentimental picturesque quality of the English-style parks so magnificently created by his master Friedrich Ludwig von Sckell, at both Schwetzingen and Nymphenburg for the King of Bavaria.

Lenné did not forsake the lessons he had learnt from Von Sckell but developed their broad lines to create the peaceful harmony of the country villas described by Pliny. On the flat land crossed by the many branches of the river Havel he re-created the atmosphere of Italy with sparsely wooded hills, shady walks running along the river's edge, pergolas, and pavilions that invite the wanderer to rest. Lenné worked at Klein-Glienicke until 1831 and at Charlottenhof from 1826 to 1843, creating the same bucolic atmosphere for both villas and for their extensions, an atmosphere in which ancient and modern Italy come together in harmony.

The fascination with Italy led architects to think again about the orangery, which had become a somewhat neglected feature by that time. Carl Gotthard Langhans, who in 1793 had completed the Brandenburg Gate, had introduced an orangery to provide a focal point in the landscaping of the new Potsdam gardens, now the Cecilienhof. The gardens were created in 1786 for Frederick William II and were to supersede Sans-Souci, which was now considered to be overly Rococo. An interesting feature of the orangery is the different style of its façades. On the south side where it looks on to the gardens the façade is perfectly traditional; however, on the east side it has an enigmatic splendour and provides a remarkable view of the lake.

Potsdam, Charlottenhof
Brandenburg
design by Karl Friedrich Schinkel, 1826
executed by Karl Friedrich Schinkel and Ludwig Persius, 1829–1840
Roman Baths and Gardener's House

Above:
garden vase
Facing page:
general view from the small lake

Left:
Karl Friedrich Schinkel
Sammlung architektonischer Entwürfe ..., 1838
perspective view of the Gardener's House

A monumental porch in the Doric style, borrowed from Boulée, forms the entrance to a "temple of botany". The doorway is guarded by the figures of two Egyptian priests and a sphinx.

In 1840, when Ludwig Persius came to build an orangery for the gardens at Klein-Glienicke he did not seek to achieve the "sublime" beloved of neo-classicists but to re-create the peaceful and domestic charm of a more familiar Italy. Here, as at Charlottenhof, where in 1829 he had completed the Roman baths started by Schinkel with a Gardener's Lodge, he returns to neat spaces and high features, such as towers or belvederes, and the unadorned simplicity that characterizes the rural dwellings of the Roman countryside. For Persius they provided an ideal solution to his more domestic projects and allowed him to avoid the somewhat cold elegance of Schinkel's villas.

Persius sought to achieve this same understatement when he was commissioned to extend the west wing of the palace at Sans-Souci by creating a new orangery. This project was continued by August Stüler and Ludwig Hesse in 1851, six years after Persius's death, and completed in 1860. By then times had changed and the 1848 revolution had been quickly repressed. The *Kronprinz*, now King Frederick William IV, wanted the orangery to symbolize the rediscoered splendour of the house of Prussia; it was to become part of a triumphal avenue leading from the palace of Sans-Souci and ending with a belvedere overlooking the city of Potsdam.

The splendour of the project dictated that the orangery become a palace. It contained the sumptuous apartments of the King's sister, Alexandra-Feodorovna, wife of Czar Nicholas I, and was also the perfect setting in which to display the forty-seven copies of the great masters that the King had ordered from his court painters.

The Italian dream culminated in a grandiose vision: the aim was to re-create both the Bramante Belvedere and Medici Villa in Rome. In 1862, to make the illusion complete, Lenné, like many architects in France and England, re-created the Renaissance gardens adjoining the orangery and the Sicilian garden below it.

FACING PAGE:
Potsdam, Cecilienhof
Brandenburg
Carl Gotthard Langhans
Orangery, 1795
recessed porch

Potsdam, Klein-Glienicke
Brandenburg
Peter Joseph Lenné
Park, 1824–1831

ABOVE:
Ludwig Persius
Orangery, 1840
RIGHT:
Ludwig Persius
Stibadium, 1840

Park of Sans-Souci
Potsdam, Brandenburg
design by Ludwig Persius, 1845
executed by August Stüler and Ludwig Hesse, 1851–1864
Orangery Palace

ABOVE:
view of the Orangery Palace from a garden terrace
FACING PAGE:
front view

LEFT:
Franz Michelis
Pfingstberg Belvedere, 1862
oil painting

Notes

Chapter 1
The Pursuit of Pleasure

1. Giovanni Boccaccio, *The Decameron*, 1350.

2. For further information on the gardens of Antiquity in the Middle East and the Mediterranean basin see Raymond Billiard, *L'Agriculture dans l'Antiquité, d'après les Géorgiques de Virgile*, Paris 1928; Pierre Grimal, *Les jardins romains à la fin de la République et aux premiers siècles de l'Empire*, Paris 1943, and Louis Hautecœur, *Les Jardins des Dieux et des Hommes*, Paris 1959.

3. Alain Rey et al., *Dictionnaire historique de la langue française*, Paris 1992.

4. Victor Loret, *Le cédratier dans l'Antiquité*, Paris 1891.

5. Pliny the Elder, *Historia Naturalis*.

6. Agostino Gallo, *Le venti giornate dell'agricoltura e de' piaceri della villa*, Venice 1569. French translation, *L'Estat et les secrets de la vraye Agriculture de Monsieur Augustin Gallo...*, Paris 1571.
In the French translation the French term "citron" [lemon] is treated as equivalent to the English term "citron", and "limon" to the lemon; "orengier"or orange tree is still spelt in its medieval form, "orenge".

7. The systematic classification of citrus fruits, the collective name given to cultivated members of the *rutaceae* family, being principally species of the genus *Citrus*, is particularly complex as it involves cultivated and hybridized forms established over thousands of years, and many different varieties.
According to Luigi Izzo, in *Storia dell'agricoltura europea, la produzione e il commercio degli agrumi*, Milan 1980, and Jean-Clause Beton, in *L'Aventure de l'orange*, Paris 1993, the principal citrus fruits cultivated today are: the citron *(Citrus medica)*; the Seville or sour orange *(Citrus aurantium bigaradia)*; the true lime *(Citrus aurantifolia)*; the bergamot orange *(Citrus bergamia)* a hybrid of the sour orange and the true lime; the lemon *(Citrus limonum)*; the sweet orange *(Citrus aurantium sinensis)*; the grapefruit *(Citrus maxima)*, which is in fact the *Citrus paradisi* or English grapefruit, the product of a hybridization of the pomelo introduced in Florida in 1823; the mandarin *(Citrus reticulata)* discovered in China and introduced into England in 1805 and its variety the clementine produced in Algeria in 1902 by Father Clément Rodier; and the kumquat *(Citrus fortunella)* discovered in China by the English botanist Robert Fortune in 1848.

8. Agostino Gallo, op. cit.

9. The role of the sour orange, the lemon, and the bergamot orange in the history of perfume manufacture is described by Nigel Groom in *The Perfume Handbook*, London 1992 and by Jean-Claude Beton in "L'orange et la parfumerie" in *L'Aventure de l'Orange*, Paris 1993.

10. F.M. Soldini, *Il reale giardino di Boboli nella sua pianta e nelle sue statue*, Florence 1789 (reprinted 1976); Francesco Gurrieri and Joan Chatfield, *Boboli Gardens*, Florence 1972.

11. In his account of the "tour" of the gardens and stately homes of Britain (1829 to 1842), and published in the form of articles (reprint, Priscilla Boniface, *In Search of English Gardens*, London 1987), John Claudius Loudon reports that in 1804 there was still an orangery with removable roof and side panels in the gardens of the Archbishop of York at Newnham Courtney.

12. Agostino Gallo, op. cit.

13. Charles VIII, *Lettres de Naples*, 28 March 1495, in *Lettres de Charles VIII*, P. Pélicier, Paris 1903.

14. Jean d'Auton, *Chroniques*, 1502, in Paul L. Jacob, *Chroniques publiées d'après le manuscrit de la bibiothèque du roi...*, 1834.

15. Martine Tissier de Mallerais, "Les jardins du château de Blois", in Jean-Marie Pérouse de Montclos, *Architecture en Région Centre*, le Guide du Patrimoine collection, Paris 1987.

16. Jean-Marie Pérouse de Montclos, "Anet", in op. cit. note 15.

17. In-depth research by Marie Thérèse Herlédan into the orangery at the Château de Meudon makes it possible for the first time to attribute the work to Le Vau. The research was published under the title "Peut-on dater l'orangerie de Meudon?", in the *Bulletin de la Société des Amis de Meudon*, no. 174, September 1987.

18. Definition given in 1694 in the first edition of the *Dictionnaire de l'Académie française*. Although the use of the word "orangerie" to refer to a building dates from the first half of the seventeenth century a definition does not appear until the publication of the French version of the dictionary (as opposed to the Latin-French version) by Pierre Richelet, *Dictionnaire françois contenant les mots et les choses*, Paris 1679–1680. This reads: "orangerie": place where orange trees are stored.
André Félibien, in his treatise *Des principes de l'Architecture, de la Sculpture, de la Peinture... avec un dictionnaire pour chacun des arts*, Paris 1676, does not mention it, although he does include words such as aviary.

19. Jacques Boyceau de la Baraudière, *Traité du jardinage selon les raisons de la nature et de l'art*, Paris 1638 and Claude Mollet, *Le Théâtre des plans et jardinage*, Paris 1652.

20. M. Valmont de Bomare, *Dictionnaire raisonné universel d'histoire naturelle*, Paris 1764, third edition revised, with additions, Paris 1776, 9 vols.

21. Jacques-François Blondel, *De la distribution des maisons de plaisance et de la décoration des édifices en général*, Paris 1737.

22. Antoine Joseph Dezallier d'Argenville, *La théorie et la pratique du jardinage*, Paris 1709. In the case of the Trianon gardens the architect, Leroy, even had the orange trees placed "in iron-covered pails that were sunk in the ground" so that the effect would be "more natural" – see Ernest de Ganay, *Les jardins de France*, Paris 1949.

23. Le Prince de Ligne, *Le coup d'œil sur Belœil*, Belœil 1781. Reprinted with introduction and notes by Count Ernest de Ganay, Paris 1922.

Chapter 2
New Directions

1. Germain Bazin, *Paradeisos ou l'Art du jardin*, Paris 1988.

2. Jean Rousset, "Le Ballet de Cour", in *La littérature de l'âge baroque en France, Circé et le paon*, Paris 1953.

3. For the Heidelberg gardens Salomon de Caus created the "moving" fountains that appeared in his work *La raison des forces mouvantes avec diverses machines tant utiles que plaisantes*, Frankfurt 1615.

4. Salomon de Caus left Heidelberg in 1620 when the Elector Palatine, Frederick V, moved to Prague and was crowned King of Bohemia. He went to live in Paris and published his work *Hortus palatinus*, in which he gives a detailed description of the gardens and future projects, of which his famous orangery was to form a part. He also illustrates a large, collapsible orangery for orange trees grown in the open ground, often referred to and confused with his other orangery design.

5. Friedrich von Schiller, *Geschichte des Dreissigjährigen Krieges*, Leipzig 1791–1793.

6. For further information on the Huguenot immigration to the German principalities see Pierre Gaxotte, *Histoire de l'Allemagne*, Paris 1975.
With particular reference to the role played by the Great Elector of Brandenburg, Frederick William, and the Edict of Potsdam of 1685 on benefits granted to protestant emigrés wishing to move to the principality, see Cyril Buffet, *Berlin*, 1993.

7. Dieter Hennebo, Alfred Hoffman, *Geschichte der deutschen Gartenkunst*, Hamburg 1962–1965, 3 vols., and Erika Neubauer, *Lustgärten des Barock*, Salzburg 1966.

8. Pierre Lafue, *La vie quotidienne des cours allemandes au XVIIIᵉ siècle*, Paris 1963.

9. Nicolas Powell, *From Baroque to Rococo, an Introduction to Austrian and German Architecture from 1580 to 1790*, London 1968; Beyer-Mielke, *Baroque Architecture in Germany*, Leipzig 1961, and Harald Keller et al., *Die Kunst des 18. Jahrhunderts*, Berlin 1971.

10. Oswald Zenkner, *Schwetzingen*, Schwetzingen 1991; Hans-Joachim Giersberg et al., *Sans-Souci*, Potsdam 1986, and Adolf Lang, *Ansbach*, Ansbach 1990.

11. Pierre Lafue, op. cit.

12. Karl Ludwig von Pöllnitz, *Nouveaux mémoires*, Amsterdam 1737. During his stay in Dresden in 1714 Pöllnitz attended the wedding of the natural son of Frederick Augustus, Hermann Maurice of Saxony, later Maréchal de France, and describes the celebrations that took place twenty years earlier in honour of Hermann Maurice's mother, the Countess Aurora of Königsmark.

13. Pierre Gaxotte, *Histoire de l'Allemagne*, Paris 1975.

14. Germain Bazin, *Destin du Baroque*, Paris 1970.

15. Elisabeth Herget, *Die Sala Terrena und der Gartensaal im deutschen Barock*, thesis published by the Johann Wolfgang Goethe University, Frankfurt 1954.

16. Pierre-Jean Remy, *Des châteaux en Allemagne*, Paris 1987.

17. The north-east side of the Zwinger, which remained open during the reign of Frederick Augustus, was used for temporary stands erected for visiting dignitaries, and was only enclosed in the nineteenth century. Between 1847 and 1854 Gottfried Semper created the Old Masters Gallery there. The façade on the town side of the Gallery opens on to the Theatre Square and faces the Opera House, also built by Semper and completed in 1878. For further information on the construction of the Zwinger see the comprehensive study by Fritz Löffer, *Der Zwinger zu Dresden*, Dresden 1981.

18. Werner Wenzel, *Die Gärten des Lothar Franz von Schönborn, Gaibach, Schloss Pommersfelden...*, 1970; Bettina Clausmeyer-Ewers and Bernd Modrow, *Historische Gärten in Hessen*, Bad Homburg 1989, and Klaus Merten, *Weikersheim*, Stuttgart 1985.

19. Pierre Gaxotte, op. cit.

Chapter 3
The Orangery Transformed

1. The English essayist Joseph Addison published his essays on the relationship between Art and Nature in *The Spectator*, a journal he founded and edited between 1711 and 1714. These essays were translated into French in 1746 in the fourth volume of the work *Le Spectateur ou Socrate moderne*, Amsterdam and Leipzig 1746–1750, 7 vols.

2. Thomas Whateley, *Observations on Modern Gardening*, London 1770. French translation by François-de-Paule Latapie, *L'Art de former les jardins modernes*, Paris 1771.

3. Marie-Madeleine Martinet, *Art et Nature en Grande-Bretagne au XVIIIᵉ siècle, de l'harmonie classique au pittoresque du premier romantisme*, Paris 1980.

4. May Woods and Arete Swartz Warren, "The England of John Evelyn" in *Glass Houses*, London 1988.

5. One of the first occasions on which the distinction appears between a greenhouse, designed for "exotic plants which could not survive the winter cold outdoors", and an orangery, "a gallery or enclosed place in which to shelter orange trees during the winter", is in

the *New and Universal Dictionary of Arts and Science*, London 1751. However, it was not until the beginning of the nineteenth century that a clear distinction would be made between these two types of protective building (see chapter 4).

6. John Hix, *The Glass House*, London 1974.

7. André Maurois, *Histoire de l'Angleterre*, Paris 1947.

8. C.M. Davies, *The History of Holland from the Beginning of the Tenth Century to the End of the Eighteenth*, London 1851, and J.L. Price, *Culture and Society in the Dutch Republic during the 17th Century*, London 1974.

9. The Oxford Physic Garden was created by the Count of Danby in 1621 but only began to function eleven years later.
In 1673 the Chelsea Physic Garden in London was inaugurated by the Society of Apothecaries but its real importance began when Sir Hans Sloane offered the Society the grounds of his Chelsea manor house, purchased in 1712, as a bequest on condition that the land should always be used for a botanical garden and only by specialists.

10. *Magnolia grandiflora* was brought back from Louisiana in 1711 by a French naval officer and presented to the owner of the Manoir de la Maillardière, near Nantes. However, it did not bloom until 1731, when it was removed from a tub in the orangery and planted out in open ground in the gardens. It was then that botanists and horticulturists "discovered" it and, incorrectly, gave this as the date when it was first introduced. See Peter Coats, *Les fleurs dans l'histoire*, Lausanne 1970.

11. Alice G.B. Lockwood, *Gardens of Colony and State. Gardens and Gardeners of the American Colonies and of the Republic before 1840*, New York 1934.

12. Philip Miller, *Gardeners' and Florists' Dictionary*, London 1724–1731. French translation, *Dictionnaire des jardiniers. Ouvrage traduit de l'anglais sur la 8ᵉ édition de Philip Miller*, Paris 1785.

13. John Kenworthy-Browne, John Harris, and Neil Stacy, *Dyrham Park*, revised and corrected, London 1991.

14. André Maurois, op. cit.

15. Kerry Downes, *Nicholas Hawksmoor*, London 1969.

16. Essays published by Joseph Addison in *The Spectator*, 21 June–3 July 1712. See note 1.

17. Jonathan Richardson, *An Argument in behalf of the Science of a Connoisseur ...*, London 1719. French translation, Jonathan Richardson, *Discours sur la Science d'un Connoisseur*, in *Traité de la Peinture*, Amsterdam, s.d.

18. Miriam Milman, "La découverte de l'objet", in *Le trompe-l'œil*, Geneva 1982.

19. Geoffrey Beard, *The Work of Robert Adam*, London 1978.
20. In 1718 Richard Bradley published *The Gentleman's and Gardener's Kalendar*, in which he devotes a chapter to greenhouses. In it he reproduces the plan by the architect Alessandro Galilei for an orangery with a glass dome designed for the Duke of Chandos. The design was reproduced in the sixth edition of his work, published in 1731 under the title *New Improvements of Planting and Gardening*.

Chapter 4
Cultivation and Collection

1. Abbé Jacques Delille, *Les Jardins ou l'Art d'embellir les paysages, poème,* Paris 1782.

2. John Evelyn noticed that the heat from stoves placed inside greenhouses made plants sick and weak and caused blemishes. He therefore proposed that a stove placed outside the greenhouse should be fed with air from within through a duct installed below ground and a grill on the wall opposite the one behind which the stove was located. The atmospheric depression thus created would be filled by the arrival of warm air from the pipes heated by the stove.

3. John Hix, "The Artificial Climate. I: Heating" op. cit. ch. III.

4. (Diderot and d'Alembert) *Encyclopédie ou Dictionnaire raisonné des sciences et des métiers*, Neuchâtel 1765. In this work the orangery is defined as "a building which in winter serves to protect orange trees and *exotic plants in general* from the cold"; the authors also recommend "heating the orangery without lighting a fire within but by passing pipes from a stove through the opening of an adjoining wall". Thus the orangery and the hot house remain very similar in both their function and their method of heating.

5. A. Davy de Virville et al., *Histoire de la botanique en France*, Paris 1954.

6. The island of Tahiti was discovered in June 1767 by Admiral Samuel Wallis, captain of the Dolphin, on which Cook had been appointed lieutenant. The following year, April 1768, Bougainville landed on the island, remaining there for two weeks. Cook returned in 1769, accompanied by Sir Joseph Banks, later to become director of the Royal Gardens at Kew; he returned again in 1773 and 1777. See Teuira Henry, *Tahiti aux temps anciens*, Paris 1951.

7. M. de Fels, *Pierre Poivre ou l'amour des épices*, Paris 1968.

8. Alice M. Coats, *The Quest for Plants. A History of the Horticultural Explorers*, London 1969.

9. Jean-Marie Morel, *Théorie des jardins,* Paris 1776.

10. Le Prince de Ligne, op. cit. ch. I.

11. B. Chevalier and B. Pincemailles, *L'Impératrice Joséphine*, Paris 1988.

12. René de Chateaubriand, *Mémoires d'outre-tombe*, published in serial form in the journal *La Presse*, 1848–1850. Full text and commentary, partly unpublished, produced by Maurice Levaillant, Paris 1948.

13. Philippe Foucault, *Le pêcheur d'orchidées, Aimé Bonpland*, Paris 1990.

14. Richard Bisgrove, *The English Garden*, 1990.

15. May Woods and Arete Swartz Warren, op. cit. ch. III.

16. Pierre Boitard, *Traité de la composition et de l'ornement des jardins*, fifth edition, Paris 1839 (first edition in 1818).

17. The term jardin d'hiver did not come into common use until the popular Jardin d'Hiver in the Champs Elysées was opened to the public in 1846.

It copied the example of the London winter gardens, the first of which was built in Regent's Park in 1842 and was used as a venue for flower shows and other events. Until then glazed extensions to country or town houses in the style of the English conservatory has still been known as serres or greenhouses. In 1831, in the novel *La Peau de Chagrin*, Balzac speaks of "a small greenhouse, a kind of room filled with flowers and on a level with the garden". See *La grande Histoire des Serres et des Jardins d'Hiver*, Bernard Marrey and Jean Pierre Monnet, Paris, s.d.

18. For the orangery at the Tuileries gardens the architect, Firmin Bourgeois, adopted the style of the conservatories built by Wyatville. However, the original purpose for which the orangery was built was soon forgotten and in 1918 it became a museum, the Musée de l'Orangerie. See Pierre Nicolas Sainte-Fare-Garnot and Emmanuel Jacquin, *Château des Tuileries*, Paris 1988.

19. When it was created in 1804 the Society had only seven members: John Wedgwood, William Forsyth, Charles Greville, R.A. Salisbury, James Dickson, and, of course, Joseph Banks and William Townsend Aiton, director and superintendent of the Royal Gardens at Kew. By its fourth meeting that same year the membership had risen to sixty. See H.R. Fletcher, *The Story of the Royal Horticultural Society*, Oxford 1969.

20. Barrie Trinder, *The Darbys of Coalbrookdale*, first edition 1974, revised with additions, Chichester (Sussex) 1991.

21. Jacqueline Fearn, *Cast Iron*, London 1990.

22. Claude Mignot, *L'Architecture au XIXᵉ siècle*, Lausanne 1983.

23. Pierre Boitard, op. cit.

24. George Mackenzie, article published in *Transactions of the Horticultural Society*, London 1817.

25. John Claudius Loudon, *Sketches of Curvilinear Hothouses*, London 1818, and *A Comparative View of the Usual and the Curvilinear Process of the Roofing of Hothouses*, London 1818.

26. G.F. Chadwick, *The Works of Sir Joseph Paxton*, London 1961.

27. Anthony Bird, *Paxton's Palace*, London 1976.

28. Pierre Boitard, op. cit., sixth edition, Paris 1859 (revised, with additions).

29. John Hix, op. cit. ch. III.

30. Loudon's publication *The Gardener's Magazine* was published from 1826 until 1843, the year of his death. In 1829 he published a second journal, *The Magazine of Natural History*, but this was by no means as successful as the first, which was frequently copied. These two journals were followed by *The Architecture Magazine* from 1834 to 1838 and *Suburban Gardener* in 1836.

31. John Claudius Loudon's account of the "tour" of the gardens and stately homes of Great Britain he made between 1829 and 1842 was published in the form of articles. These were reprinted: Priscilla Boniface, *In Search of English Gardens*, London 1987.

32. Honoré de Balzac, *La fausse maîtresse*, Paris 1842.

CHAPTER 5
Final Splendour

1. François Loyer, *Le siècle de l'industrie*, Geneva 1983.

2. Humphry Repton, *Sketches and Hints on Landscape Gardening*, London 1794.

3. Richard Bisgrove, op. cit. ch. IV.

4. Priscilla Boniface, op. cit. ch. IV.

5. André Maurois, op. cit. ch. III.

6. Nathaniel Wallich discovered *Amherstia nobilis* in 1826 in the courtyard of a Burmese monastery near Ava, the royal seat of the Burmese monarch, while on an expedition organized to negotiate a peace treaty with the King. It was cultivated in the botanical garden at Calcutta and named in honour of Lady Amherst, the wife of the India's governor general, who had a keen interest in botany.

7. Nadine Beautheac and François-Xavier Bouchart, *L'Europe exotique*, Paris 1985.

8. Ludwig von Zanth, *Die Wilhelma, maurische Villa*, Leipzig 1855.

9. Owen Jones was appointed chief of works for the construction of the Crystal Palace. He was greatly influenced by his research into polychromy, carried out during his various trips abroad and to Spain in particular. For Paxton's great aisle he created a system of decoration based entirely on the interplay of colour. See Robin Middleton and David Watkin, *Architettura dell' Ottocento*, Milan 1980.

10. Michel Le Bris, "Les Orients de l'âme ou le lieu de l'art", in *Journal du Romantisme*, Geneva 1981,

11. François Loyer, op. cit.

12. Margheria, dialect form of the Piedmontese word *margaria*, meaning farm. See Mirella Macera et al., *Il parco de Racconigi*, Racconigi 1989.

13. "Do not all these buildings charm the eye with their simple and pleasant forms?" writes Jean-Nicolas Louis Durand in *Précis des leçons d'architecture données à l'École polytechnique*, published 1802–1805. He is one of the first to praise the charm of these country dwellings, which would soon become part of the varied repertoire of the garden pavilion.

Bibliography

ARCHER R., *Early Views of India. The Picturesque Journeys of Thomas and William Daniell 1785–1794*, London 1980.

ARNEVILLE M.B. d', *Parcs et jardins sous le Premier Empire*, Paris 1981.

BACHMANN E., *Wurtzbourg, le palais des princes-évêques*, French edition Munich 1982.

BAJARD S., BENCINI R., *Villas et jardins de Toscane*, Paris 1992.

BEARD G., *Stucco and Decorative Plasterwork in Europe*, London 1983.

BLUNT W., *The Art of Botanical Illustration*, London 1950, reprinted 1994.

BORSI F., PAMPALONI G., *Ville e giardini*, Novara 1984.

BURDET H., et al., *Ouvrages botaniques anciens. Catalogue des ouvrages prélinnéens de la Bibliothèque des Conservatoire et Jardin botaniques de la Ville de Genève*, Geneva 1985.

BUREAUD G., *Les masques*, Paris 1948.

BUSSADORI P., *Il giardino e la scena*, Treviso 1986.

CANDOLLE A. DE, *Origine des plantes cultivées*, Paris 1896.

CHAMBERS W., *Plans, Elevations, Sections and Perspective Views of the Gardens and Buildings at Kew...*, London 1763.

CLIFFORD J., *Capability Brown*, Haverfordwest 1974.

CONDER S., JOHNSON D., *Conservatories and Garden Rooms*, London 1990.

CRUICKSHANK D., *A Guide to the Georgian Buildings of Britain and Ireland*, London 1985.

DETERVILLE P., *Châteaux de la plaine de Caen et du Cinglais*, Condé-sur-Noireau 1991.

DUVAL M., *La planète des fleurs*, Paris 1977.

FLEURENT M., *Le monde secret des jardins*, Paris 1987.

FUSCO R., *L'architettura dell'Ottocento*, Turin 1980.

GALLESIO G., *Traité du Citrus*, Paris 1871.

GLOAG J., *Mr. Loudon's England*, London 1970.

GROMORT G., *L'art des jardins*, Paris 1934.

HARDFIELD M., *The English Landscape Garden*, Haverfordwest, new edition 1988.

HASLICK P., *Greenhouse and Conservatory Construction and Heating*, London 1907.

HEPPER F.M., *Royal Botanic Gardens, Kew. Gardens for Science and Pleasure*, London 1982.

HINZ G., *Peter Joseph Lenné*, Berlin 1937.

KAISER B. and R., *L'amour des jardins, célébré par les écrivains*, Paris 1986.

KENNEDY J., *A Treatise upon Planting, Gardening and the Management of the Hot-House*, York 1776.

KOHLMAIER G. and von SARTORY B., *Houses of Glass. A Nineteenth-Century Building Type*, London 1986. Originally *Das Glashaus. Bautypus des 19. Jahrhunderts*, Munich 1981.

KOPPELKAMM S., *Glasshouses and Wintergardens of the Nineteenth Century*, London 1982.

KUSAK D., *Lednice*, Prague 1986.

LÉGER C., *Redouté et son temps*, Paris 1945.

MCINTOSH C., *The Greenhouse, Hot-House and Stove*, London 1838.

MIDDLETON R., WATKIN D., *Architettura dell'Ottocento*, Milan 1980.

MILDE K., *Die Neorenaissance in der deutschen Architektur des 19. Jahrhunderts*, Munich 1974.

MOORE P., *Margam Orangery*, West Glamorgan 1976.

MOTT G., *Follies and Pleasure Pavilions*, New York 1989.

NEUMANN W., *Art de construire et de gouverner les serres*, Paris 1844.

PINAULT M., *Le peintre et l'histoire naturelle*, Paris 1990.

POMIAN KRZYSZTOF, *Collectioneurs, amateurs et curieux. Paris, Venise: XVIe–XVIIIe siècle*, Paris 1987.

PONTVILLE M. DE, *Le manoir de La Luzerne à Bernières-sur-mer et Jacques Moisant de Brieux*, communication published in *Mémoires de l'Académie des Sciences, Arts et Belles-Lettres de Caen*, volume XXX, 1992.

Potsdamer Schlösser und Gärten, Bau- und Gartenkunst vom 17. bis 20. Jahrhundert, Schlösser und Gärten Potsdam-Sanssouci exhibition catalogue 1993.

RAMBOSSON J., *Histoire et légendes des plantes utiles*, Paris 1871.

REISINGER CLAUS, *Der Schlossgarten zu Schwetzingen*, Heidelberg 1987.

RISSO L., *Histoire naturelle des orangers*, Paris 1818.

ROBERSON W., *Collection de différentes espèces de serres chaudes*, 1798.

ROBINSON J.M., *The Wyatts. An Architectural Dynasty*, Oxford 1979.

SCHAUB F., *Berühmte Gärten in Franken*, Würzburg 1984.

SCHULZ E. VON, *Die Wilhelma in Stuttgart, ein Beispiel orientalisierender Architektur im 19. Jahrhundert und ihr Architekt Karl Ludwig von Zanth*, thesis, Tübingen 1976.

SCKELL F. L. VON, *Beiträge zur bildenden Gartenkunst für angehende Gartenkünstler und Liebhaber*, Munich 1818, reprinted Worms 1982.

SEILER M., *Die Entwicklungsgeschichte des Landschaftsgardens Klein-Glienicke 1796–1883*, thesis, Hamburg 1986.

STROUD D., *Humphry Repton*, London 1962.

SUMMERSON J., *The Life and Works of John Nash, Architect*, London 1980.

TSCHIRA A., *Orangerien und Gewächshäuser. Ihre Entwicklung in Deutschland*, Berlin 1939.

ULRICH R.M., *Glas-Eisenarchitektur. Pflanzenhäuser des 19. Jahrhunderts*, Worms 1989.

VILMORIN, JEAN BAPTISTE DE, *Le jardin des hommes. Vagabondage à travers l'origine et l'histoire des plantes cultivées*, Paris 1991.

WACKER J. ET AL., *Das Chinesische Haus im Park von Sanssouci*, Berlin 1993.

WITTKOWER R., *Palladio and English Palladianism*, London 1974.

ILLUSTRATIONS

© Unless otherwise indicated all photographs of sites and documents are by Michel Saudan.

Paintings, drawings, engravings, treatises and illustrated works

Index